THE NON-PROJECT MANAGER'S GUIDE TO

PROJECT MANAGEMENT

Sam Buah

BSc, MSc, MAPM

Foreword by
Prof. Damian O'Doherty

A Comprehensive Guide for the
APM Project Fundamentals Qualification

Grosvenor House
Publishing Limited

This book is published by
Grosvenor House Publishing Ltd
Link House
140 The Broadway, Tolworth, Surrey, KT6 7HT.
www.grosvenorhousepublishing.co.uk

A CIP record for this book
is available from the British Library

ISBN 978-1-83975-233-9

DEDICATION

To my parents Mr & Mrs. J.E Buah, you raised me up so I can be the best version of myself, I remember the many years of sacrifice and huge investment into my education. Thank you.

Also, to my sister, Gladys Buah. You have always believed in my ability even when I did not see it myself. Thank you for many years of sacrifice. I would not have been here without your help.

And to you, my little brother Jason Buah and your wife, Enjema, you both look up to me in many ways, so I hope this book will be an inspiration to you. Keep pressing on. All things are possible.

And to all those who have a dream and aspiration, keep believing and pressing. It takes time but will certainly happen if you don't give up.

FOREWORD

Can one eat an elephant whole? Sometimes, notably for those outside the profession, project management appears to make as much sense as this question. There is a kind of wisdom available for those willing to invest the time in such conundrums of course, but it is wisdom absolutely essential for anyone who wants to make a go of project management. And it's the kind of wisdom out of which Sam Buah has written this most illuminating and engaging of books about a topic which is, frankly – 'How's your project management?' – not exactly something which strikes most people as a good conversation starter. You can forget PRINCE2! That's a formal qualification, a show window in which to display status and project certified reassurance – an absolutely essential resource to have at your disposal. But let's get behind the public front to look at what is really needed of a project manager. Let's take a look at those things you always wanted to know about project management but were afraid to ask.

This book will teach you all you need to know in order to begin project management. For those with some experience, it will help advance or improve your mastery of this devilishly tricky management specialism. And it's a pleasure to read. You will want to spend time with Sam. He has the professional and life experience, and the rare combination of practical knowledge, academic expertise, patience and guile, that is the hallmark of people who get things done. He has worked on big projects and small projects. He can put a bridge up, build an airport, and take one down.

I was once told that a project manager is someone who does nothing but without whom nothing would get done. It's another one of those Zen-like koans that bears fruit only slowly and after much experience, mistake-making, and long drawn-out thought and reflection. The problem is that there is a rich gamut of specialist and arcane vocabulary surrounding project management that is intimidating and incomprehensible but behind which the young and incompetent typically hide their lack of expertise. "Have you got your product breakdown structure?" you will hear them say; "Why not adopt the arrow-diagrammed method on your critical path structure?". Suits you, sir! Or, "You'll probably need change control for that." "Perhaps it's best to get yourself a PESTLE analysis done?" More often than not it's flimflam, snake oil, mantra, hustle or gyp. The art of the grifter. You know these people... snooping around the corridors of corporate power, collars up, ears buried in their iPhone, whispering, black-market spivs and spin doctors.

Sam explains each item of project management speak in an easy and accessible manner from which it is quick to learn and memorise. The trick here is that Sam is able to talk in two languages, or to two audiences, at once – those with considerable project management experience and those who know nothing about it. Maybe you need to deal with project managers. Or you are thinking about exploring the possibility of becoming a project manager. This is the book for you. Whether you are buying a car, planning a vacation or building an international space station, you will need to be a very good project manager. I think this is what the reader will find most engaging about this book, whether you know anything or nothing about project management.

It is a pleasure to write this foreword for Sam. I was asked to write it because I once spent two and a half years doing an anthropological study of project managers at Manchester Airport Group, where Sam also works. In the kind of fieldwork I do, one has to try and acquire the skills of those one is studying. This meant I had to pass the PRINCE2 project management exams! "A professor!" I was teased. "You'll pass that with flying colours." I am here to tell you I barely managed to scrape a pass – and that after spending weeks and weeks of sleepless nights reading the PRINCE2 manual. And yet, back at university I am alone in having that qualification, even amongst those who are academic experts in the field. Some colleagues, who shall remain nameless, profess project management by day but go home to houses falling down, with half-finished timbers, faulty air-handling units, mechanical and electrical scope creep, and voids instead of soffits. How much they could learn from this book! It's another elephant in the room that those who claim expertise in project management are amongst the worst practitioners or educators.

You will learn much from this book, and if you're lucky enough you will work out in your own way why the elephant is an endangered species and what you can do about that as a project manager.

Damian O'Doherty
Professor of Management and Organisation
Alliance Manchester Business School
University of Manchester

TABLE OF CONTENTS

LIST OF FIGURES

LIST OF TABLES

ACKNOWLEDGEMENT

The writing of this book would not have been possible without the effort and assistance of so many individuals. I have learnt from each one of them through our conversations and from my own observations.

Ultimately, I thank my immediate family for believing and supporting the vision of writing this book. You are the ones who felt the direct impact while I spent long hours and sacrificed every little time I should have spent with you to write this book. Special thanks go to my wife Victoria and my children Anna-Darlene, Andrew, Joel and Jesse. You have been of great help on this journey, especially you, my adorable twins, Joel and Jesse. You never ceased to show interest in the book from the first day you found out. I will always remember your trademark query, "Daddy, have you finished the book?" and my response was always, "Nearly finished." Now I can proudly say my work is done.

And to all of you who played a role in diverse ways in the writing of this book, I am forever grateful. The list is endless, hence if I ever spoke to you about this book, please note that you are the very person I say a big thank you to.

Finally, I want to thank all my colleagues at Manchester Airport, especially Brad Miller, for supporting and assisting with various contacts. Also, to all other colleagues at Manchester Airport who helped in any way to make the writing of this book possible. Special thanks go to Simon Wood, Gary Craven, Kevin Seagrave, David Freeston, Rebecca Leyland, and Daniel Molyneux for all your help.

I also wish to thank my sister Tina Thompson and my friend Nana Yaa Mensah of Kedaph Schoolwear for the continued encouragement.

My final thanks go to Rev. Clarence Acquaye and Rev. Edward Asong for inspiring and cheering me on in many ways.

ABOUT THE AUTHOR

Sam Buah is a seasoned project manager with well over 15 years of project management experience. This spans across the rail, transport and aviation industries, involving different kinds of projects such as design and build, construction, and refurbishment and security, among others.

In recent months, Sam has dedicated his time to focusing on leading programmes of small- to medium-sized projects, areas of project management which are unique in their delivery. These have opened doors to opportunities for him to have a much deeper knowledge and understanding of managing minor projects.

Sam has been working with and supporting many non-project managers and tailoring project management techniques and processes to suit each individual minor project, while at the same time not overlooking health and safety requirements.

Besides delivering projects, Sam is also a passionate trainer, an ability and skill that comes naturally to him. For the passion of sharing his knowledge, Sam always finds the time and opportunity to be involved in helping non-project managers to fully embrace and understand the need for and benefits of project management.

This is high on Sam's list of priorities and it has become his vision to embark on a series of training sessions and workshops to promote the use of project management among non-project managers and project managers.

INTRODUCTION

During my years of managing projects, I have had the opportunity to work with people with different levels of knowledge of, and experience in, project management.

The most fascinating have been while overseeing the delivery of minor projects. This aspect of project management has been an eye-opener indeed. Small projects are unique in their own right. They nearly always require their own level of rigour and scrutiny different from a large project.

Projects that appear to be small and easy to manage could lend themselves to escaping the typical project management processes.

Nonetheless, and surprisingly, if a small project goes wrong, it can potentially have a catastrophic impact on any business regardless of the value of that project.

I have seen many people become caught out while attempting **small projects** simply because they failed to apply the appropriate level of rigour and process. They did too much, too little or nothing at all.

I have also seen many **non-project managers** attempt the delivery of small projects and ignore fundamental steps simply because they assume them to be not important or were genuinely not aware of what to do or how to manage a project. It may well be an issue of time pressure forcing shortcuts.

This book was written to equip **non-project managers** with the right knowledge, skills, techniques and appropriate tools to efficiently and effectively manage or get involved in projects.

It is intended to promote project management understanding and offer practical tips to anyone who desires to acquire project management knowledge.

Many people think of projects as only construction, IT activities or complex endeavours that require a specialist to manage. The truth is that most of us get involved in projects without even realising. Our life activities are full of project management processes and, knowingly or unknowingly, we apply these processes.

By reading this book thoroughly and completing all the relevant exercises, you will emerge equipped with valuable knowledge on project management. You will have the confidence to get involved in project delivery or attempt to manage small and simple projects with little or no help.

Sam Buah
Author
Manchester, UK, 2021

WHO SHOULD READ THIS BOOK?

✓ Anyone with little or no knowledge of or experience in project management.

✓ Anyone who is a manager, within the leadership team, a project sponsor, etc. who from time to time is involved in project management.

✓ Individuals/self-employed, small business owners and managers who are interested in gaining more understanding of project management.

✓ Anyone interested in applying the techniques and principles of project management to their day-to-day activities.

✓ Anyone considering project management as a career change but wants to understand more before deciding.

✓ Anyone who wants project management processes simplified.

✓ Experienced project managers who wish to refresh their knowledge on project management basics.

✓ This book also aligns with the Association for Project Management (APM) Project Fundamentals Qualification (PFQ) syllabus. It can be used as a study guide for preparing towards the PFQ qualification based on the APM Body of Knowledge 7th edition.

LEARNING OBJECTIVES

The APM Project Fundamentals Qualification (PFQ) syllabus assesses the key elements of the project management life cycle and covers knowledge areas from the APM Body of Knowledge. The latest APM Body of Knowledge is the seventh edition published in 2019 by the Association for Project Management.

CHAPTER 1 Overview of project management	By the end of this chapter you should be able to: – Define the term 'project' – Outline the project limitations – State the differences between a project and business as usual – Define the term 'project management' – State the key purpose of project management – Define the terms 'programme management' and 'portfolio management' and their relationship with project management – State some of the reasons why a project can fail
CHAPTER 2 Factors that influence projects	By the end of this chapter you should be able to: – Explain why projects are affected by their environment – Explain what is meant by the project environment/context – Describe why PESTLE analysis might be used by a project manager
CHAPTER 3 Project roles and responsibilities	By the end of this chapter you should be able to: – Outline the roles and responsibilities of the project sponsor – Outline the roles and responsibilities of the project manager – Outline the roles and responsibilities of the following: project governance, project team members, end users, product owner and the project management office

CHAPTER 4 **Understanding project life cycles**	By the end of this chapter you should be able to: – Define the term 'project life cycle' – State the phases of a typical project life cycle – Use a sketch to demonstrate a typical project life cycle – Identify reasons for structuring projects into phases – List some of the key activities within each cycle phase
CHAPTER 5 **Establishing the project need (the why)**	By the end of this chapter you should be able to: – Outline the importance of establishing the project need – Define the term 'benefit management' – Distinguish between different types of benefits – Identify and group project benefits – Explain smart project benefits
CHAPTER 6 **Engaging the stakeholders**	By the end of this chapter you should be able to: – Explain who stakeholders are – State some of the techniques for identifying stakeholders – Sketch a simple stakeholder grid to demonstrate power and interest – Explain the meaning of 'stakeholder management plan' – Explain why communicating with stakeholders is important
CHAPTER 7 **How to justify the 'why' for the project**	By the end of this chapter you should be able to: – Outline the purpose and typical content of a business case – Explain the role of a project sponsor and project manager in relation to developing a business case
CHAPTER 8 **The project management plan (PMP)**	By the end of this chapter you should be able to: – State the main purpose of a project management plan – Define who is involved in the creation of the project management plan – List the typical content of a project management plan – Outline the stakeholders of a project management plan – Explain why the project management plan needs to be approved, owned and shared

CHAPTER 9 **Managing quality**	**By the end of this chapter you should be able to:** – Define the term 'quality' – Outline the purpose of quality management – Define the term 'quality planning' – Define the term 'quality control' – Outline the purpose of quality assurance
Chapter 10 **Understanding the project requirements**	**By the end of this chapter you should be able to:** – Define the term 'requirement' – Define the term 'requirement management' – Outline the steps involved in writing a good project requirement – Explain why the project manager needs to develop SMART requirements
CHAPTER 11 **Understanding the project scope**	**By the end of this chapter you should be able to:** – Define the term 'scope management' – Differentiate between scope management within linear projects and scope – Describe how product breakdown structures (PBS) and work breakdown structures (WBS) are used to illustrate the required scope of work – Outline how a project manager would use cost breakdown structures (CBS), organisational breakdown structures (OBS) and the responsibility assignment matrix (RAM)
CHAPTER 12 **Sequencing the project activities**	**By the end of this chapter you should be able to:** – State the purpose of scheduling – State the purpose of critical path analysis – State the purpose of milestones – Define the term 'timeboxing'
CHAPTER 13 **Promoting project success**	**By the end of this chapter you should be able to:** – Explain the term 'success criteria' – Explain key performance indicators, with examples – Explain success factors and give examples – Differentiate between success factors and critical success factors – Explain why establishing success criteria is important at the start, during and at handover of a project

CHAPTER 14 Understanding estimating	By the end of this chapter you should be able to: – Explain estimating – Explain why estimates are important when managing projects – Explain the different estimating techniques – State typical estimating methods (including analytical, analogous, parametric) – Outline the purpose of estimating funnel – Explain the relationship between estimating funnel and project phases – Explain why estimates can be better and more accurate as the project progresses through the life cycle stages
CHAPTER 15 Understanding configuration	By the end of this chapter you should be able to: – Define the term 'configuration management' – Stage the steps involved in managing the configuration of a product – Outline the activities in a typical configuration management process (including planning, identification, control, status accounting and verification audit) – Explain the relationship between change control and configuration management
CHAPTER 16 Dealing with changes	By the end of this chapter you should be able to: – Define the term 'change' – Explain what is meant by 'change control' – Explain what goes into a typical change-control process – Explain how changes affect project scope – Understand who is responsible for managing changes
CHAPTER 17 How to manage resources	By the end of this chapter you should be able to: – Explain 'project resources' and 'resource management' – Understand the types of resources and give examples – Understand the techniques used in managing resources – Explain resource levelling and resource smoothing
CHAPTER 18 Procurement	By the end of this chapter you should be able to: – Explain procurement – Define the term 'contract' and when it is appropriate to use

CHAPTER 19 **Dealing with risks**	**By the end of this chapter you should be able to:** – Define the term 'risk' – Explain the purpose of risk management – Outline the stages of a typical risk management process (including identification, analysis, response and closure) – Describe the use of risk registers
CHAPTER 20 **Dealing with issues**	**By the end of this chapter you should be able to:** – Define the term 'issue' – Outline the purpose of issue management – Differentiate between an issue and a risk – State the stages of an issue resolution process
CHAPTER 21 **Understanding communication**	**By the end of this chapter you should be able to:** – Define the term 'communication' – Outline the advantages of different communication methods (including face-to-face, physical, virtual) – Outline the disadvantages of different communication methods (including face-to-face, physical, virtual) – Outline the content of a communication plan – Explain the benefits, to a project manager, of a communication plan
CHAPTER 22 **Understanding leadership**	**By the end of this chapter you should be able to:** – Define the term 'leadership' – Outline the challenges to a project manager when developing and leading a project team
CHAPTER 23 **Understanding the power of teamwork**	**By the end of this chapter you should be able to:** – Define the term 'project team' – Outline how a project manager can use models to assist team development (including Belbin and Tuckman)
CHAPTER 24 **Projects and the regulatory framework**	**By the end of this chapter you should be able to:** – Outline why the project manager may have to understand the legal framework when managing projects – State some of the main legal framework a project may have to abide by
CHAPTER 25 **Project reviews**	**By the end of this chapter you should be able to:** – Explain the purpose of project reviews – List and explain the different types of reviews

CHAPTER 26 Project reporting and information management	By the end of this chapter you should be able to: – Explain why reporting is important in project management – Explain the different types of reporting – Outline the purpose and benefits of project progress reporting
Appendix 1 Useful checklist	This last chapter summarises, in the form of prompt lists/questions, what should be considered/remembered at each life cycle stage. It is a summary of the key points discussed in this book.
Appendix 2 Step-by-step guide to managing a simple project	This is a step-by-step guide for managing a project. The chapters in the book are not necessarily arranged in a sequential order of how a project is managed. This chapter can be used as a reference guide to help you manage a project in a step-by-step method following the relevant chapters in the book.
Appendix 3 Project examples for discussion	This appendix gives you examples of projects you can use for group discussion and exercises.

Case study topic

Humanitarian support for displaced families

You have recently heard in the news the devastating impact a typhoon has had on a coastal town in Asia. Buildings and houses have been severely battered by heavy rain and wind. At least **50,000 residents** have been evacuated from the waterfront and mountainous regions over fears of flooding, storm waves, and landslides.

It is estimated that 40 people died as the typhoon tore through the town. Houses, offices, school buildings and health facilities, among others, have all been destroyed. There are growing concerns about the welfare of all the families who have been displaced, especially the children.

It is estimated that the total rebuilding cost of the town will approach millions of US dollars and will take several years.

The situation is very alarming given the scale of damage and the impact it is having on the people. The community has called on humanitarian agencies and governments around the world to come to its aid.

The UK government has pledged to make available up to **£100,000** to a humanitarian agency you work for. The objective is to provide immediate relief to some of the most distressed and displaced families.

Your organisation has been selected to deliver this project by providing this humanitarian support. You have up to three months to plan, mobilise and execute this relief mission given the urgency and criticality.

You are the project manager with a team tasked to make this happen.

How will you plan and execute this relief mission given all the constraints and success criteria identified?

CHAPTER 1

OVERVIEW OF PROJECT MANAGEMENT

By the end of this chapter you should be able to:

- Define the term 'project'
- Outline the project limitations
- State the differences between a project and business as usual
- Define the term 'project management'
- State the key purpose of project management
- Define the terms 'programme management' and 'portfolio management' and their relationship with project management
- State some of the reasons why a project can fail

1.1 Project management in our day-to-day activities

Naturally we plan and manage the amount of money available to us and find creative ways to get the maximum value for the money we spend, whether it is our day-to-day grocery shopping, making that big purchase or planning an event, etc.

Ever faced with having insufficient funds to spend?

Have you ever had to carry out a task, a piece of work, or accomplish something with a limited budget?

Did you have to find creative ways or apply specific skills and strategies to spend within your budget? Think about that holiday, trip, shopping, wedding, party, etc.

We are all faced with similar financial situations regularly and so does the project manager who has to deliver projects within a set budget by adopting project management processes and methods to deliver within that agreed budget.

Ever faced with having insufficient time to complete something?

What about having to complete an activity, assignment, task, etc. by a specific deadline?

Did you have to plan and organise yourself and your resources to meet this deadline? Most likely your answer is yes. Projects also operate in the same way; they are constrained by time, which means the project manager must plan and be proactive to complete projects by an expected date.

Ever felt uncertain about something you wanted to do?

What about doing or attempting something you have not tried before? Something with lots of unknowns (risks)?

Maybe you were worried about what could go wrong or the fact that it was your first attempt, yet you found ways to overcome those uncertainties.

Think about that holiday to the place you have never been before, your first attempt at painting and decorating, or even cooking that meal you have never tried before. All of these carry a degree of uncertainty which must be managed.

Project management is similar in its delivery as it attempts to bring into existence something unique. Just like any new venture, there will always be lots of **unknowns/ uncertainties** to deal with and the project manager plans to mitigate or reduce the likelihood of these and/or their consequences.

So, what next?

If you answered YES to any of the above questions, then the good news is that you already know and can apply some project management principles and methods, though you may not have formalised your processes as a project manager would do.

As a matter of fact, project management has been in existence for thousands of years – from the Egyptian era through to the construction of the Great Wall of China.

It is, however, only fairly recently, during the 21st century, that project principles and techniques were officially formalised and developed to what we have today.

It can therefore be concluded that, regardless of what we do, we all apply project management techniques and principles without even realising. In effect, project management is not new to us, but you may not have formalised and documented your processes like a project manager does.

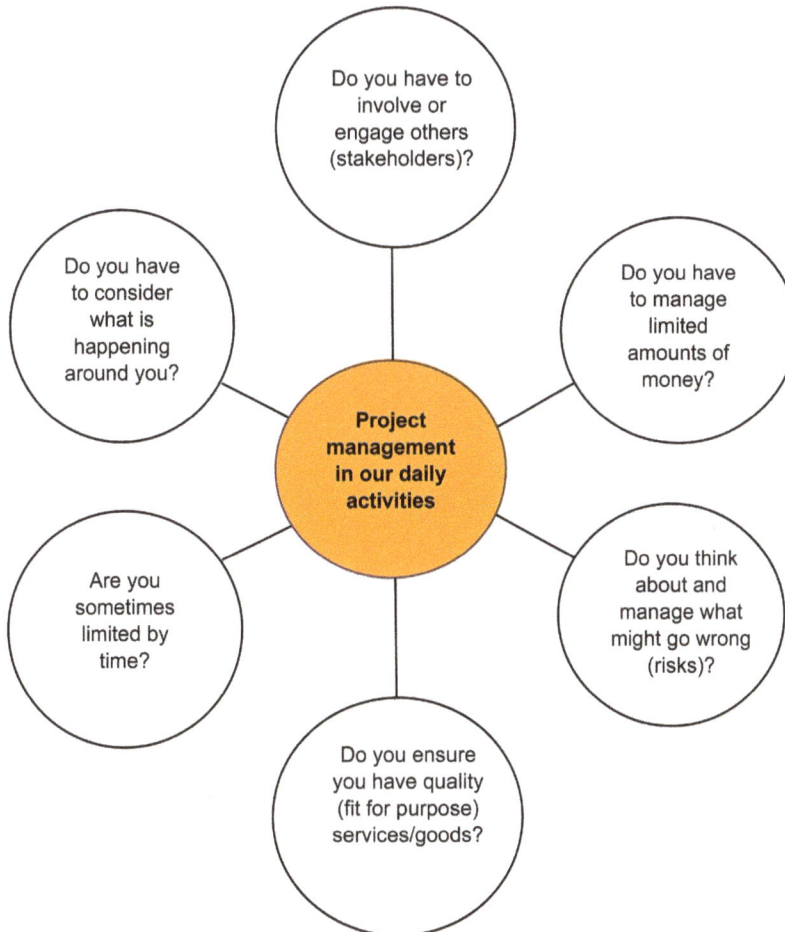

Figure 1.1 Project management in our daily activities

1.2 What is a project?

> **A project** is an activity that is temporary and undertaken to bring about a notable or unique change. The change should ultimately lead to benefits.

1.3 Project characteristics

Projects are temporary

Projects are **temporary** because they are limited by time (started and completed within a set period) to achieve **specific goals and objectives.**

In a more simplified explanation, one can say projects are made up of several activities that must be completed within a specified timeframe.

Projects are unique

Projects are **unique** because they result in new product(s) or service(s) that have not previously existed in the exact same form.

It does not only mean creating something new from scratch but could also be an improvement to an existing product or service where the improvement represents something new or unique.

Projects lead to benefits

Project **benefits** are the tangible improvements delivered by the project. In effect, every project is undertaken to result in positive improvement. Projects are not delivered simply because it is a nice thing to do. Projects are delivered with benefits in mind which should be quantifiable after the project is complete. An example of benefit is to reduce customer waiting times by 50%, expand the capacity of a retail space and double the profit over two years.

Projects have limitations

Projects are always expected to deliver outputs that should meet agreed **requirements.** These agreed requirements, if delivered, will ultimately lead to deriving the expected benefits for the project.

By their nature, projects are limited or constrained by: **time, cost, quality and risks.**

This means that you will never have unlimited amounts of time or money to deliver your projects, yet you will be expected to deliver to a certain quality using the agreed amounts of money and time. Projects also have a lot of uncertainties with their delivery which must be managed as part of the project.

As a matter of fact, whenever there is a change to any one of these limitations, for example if the available time is shortened, available budget cut, etc., this can affect how and what is delivered by the project.

Projects come in various sizes and complexities

There are several types and kinds of projects, ranging from industry specific projects, such as construction, infrastructure and refurbishment projects, to IT, retail projects, and many more.

Example: building a new bus station, a new railway line, renovating a house, introducing new computer software, fitting out a new shop, etc. are all projects.

Projects come in various sizes and with different levels of complexity. Some are simple and straightforward, taking a few hours or days to **plan, execute** and **hand over.** Others may take several months or years to plan, execute and hand over.

For example, constructing a new bridge across a river could be classified as a large and complex project which will be different from a small and simple project like painting and decorating a one-bedroom house.

Whether a project is simple or complex, has a long or short duration, is small or large, they all share the same **project characteristics.**

Examples:

- If the amount of money available for the *humanitarian project* suddenly gets withdrawn or reduced, the project may not be completed, or if completed may affect time, cost and quality.
- If there is suddenly no time to complete the work, it will affect the product. Maybe the work cannot be finished or cannot be done properly.
- Sometimes an unforeseen event can stop the project or force it to change its course, e.g. financial risks, health and safety risks, reputational risks, etc.

Managing a project means using **processes** and **methods** supported by your **knowledge, skills** and **experience** to balance these main **constraints.**

Good project management means **balancing** the project constraints in such a way that a change in one or more constraints will not have a significant impact on the expected project output or deliverables.

The project manager must skilfully balance the project **risks, cost, quality** and **time** using relevant techniques and processes to deliver the expected output that meets the requirements of the stakeholders and customers.

It may be practically impossible to achieve a perfect project; however, the project manager will be expected to achieve the **optimum balance**.

Sometimes, to deliver a project to an unmovable **deadline** and **cost** may require a compromise with one or more of the project constraints.

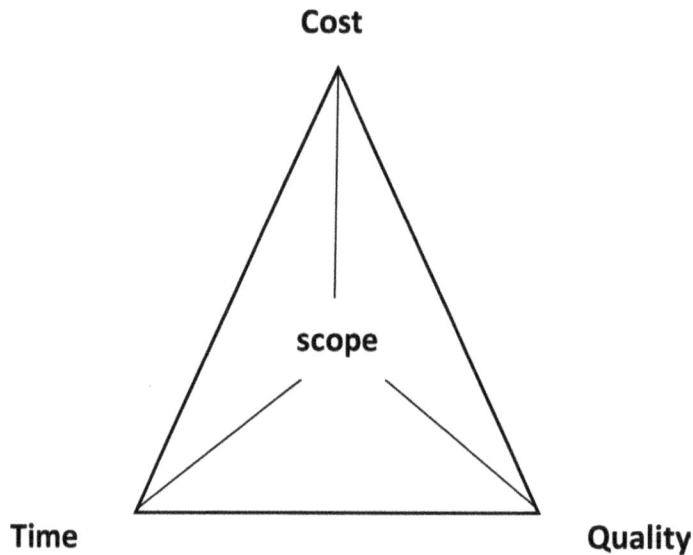

Figure 1.2 The project triangle

In summary:

☐ Projects introduce change
☐ Projects deliver specific products/services
☐ Every project delivers a planned set of outputs that deliver benefits
☐ Projects are divided and completed in stages called a life cycle
☐ Projects are delivered with an agreed budget from the start
☐ Projects have agreed start and finish dates

Table 1.1 Why projects fail sometimes

Why projects fail sometimes
When the project requirements are not clear
When the success of the completed project means something different to the stakeholders
Agreeing to completion and/or starting dates and costs which are not realistic
Not following any plan or process – you just think on your feet and do as you go
Unable to engage with the people who matter on the project (stakeholders)
Not dealing with project risks appropriately
Ineffective communication – stakeholders do not know what is happening
Inability to find and procure the right services, service providers, contractors, etc. needed for the project
Not dealing with project issues properly when they arise
Ignoring lessons from past and similar projects
Ignoring conflicts within the team or not dealing with them properly
Poor leadership
Not dealing with project changes appropriately by assessing the impact these have on cost, time and quality.

1.4 Projects versus business as usual

Table 1.2 Projects versus business as usual

Projects	Business as usual
Have defined scope and deliverables	Is the continuous management of what has already been delivered
Deliver benefits	Makes use of the benefits of the project
Are broken and delivered in steps called the life cycle phases/stages	Is a continuous improvement of the day-to-day business operations
Are constrained by time	Is not constrained by time with specific start and finish dates
Have start and finish dates	May appear as a project, however it is not constrained by time

Projects	Business as usual
Usually experts are called upon for the duration of the project and the team disbanded on completion	Follows repeated processes with the same team, and the team continues unless someone leaves
Usually have risks associated with them	Will usually be risk averse and operate with minimal or no risk

1.5 What is project management?

> **Project management** is 'the application of processes, methods, knowledge, skills and experience to achieve specific objectives for change' - (Murray-Webster, Dalcher and Association for Project Management, 2019)

You may have asked yourself the question: **Why bother with project management?**

A good overview and understanding of projects and project management opens the door to a new set of skills and knowledge for turning ideas, problems and opportunities into beneficial outputs.

Project management is a specialist discipline which equips practitioners with a good understanding and awareness of the necessary processes and methods required to manage projects.

Project management has become very popular in recent times as many organisations and individuals choose to adopt project management **principles** and **methods** to accomplish tasks and bring about positive and/or beneficial change.

Turning ideas into **outputs** that ultimately result in **benefits** does not just happen. A systematic effort and application of specific processes and methods are required in order to achieve the desired outputs. This is the discipline of **project management.**

In a more formal sense one can say that project management involves a process of: **defining, planning, monitoring** and **controlling** project activities in order to deliver the agreed outputs/outcomes.

This means that during project management, an idea will be nurtured, assessed, planned and delivered.

Project management uses the idea of careful planning to bring into reality what was planned. This idea will be brought into existence using the minimum amount of resource, budget and time as is possible.

Project management brings value to organisations and individuals who adopt the processes and methods because it follows tried and tested methods and processes.

Project management is about proactively managing project risks by exploiting opportunities for the benefit of the project and mitigating what can negatively affect the project.

Project management is about managing changes that may happen to a project and ensuring that these do not have a catastrophic impact on the project outcome.

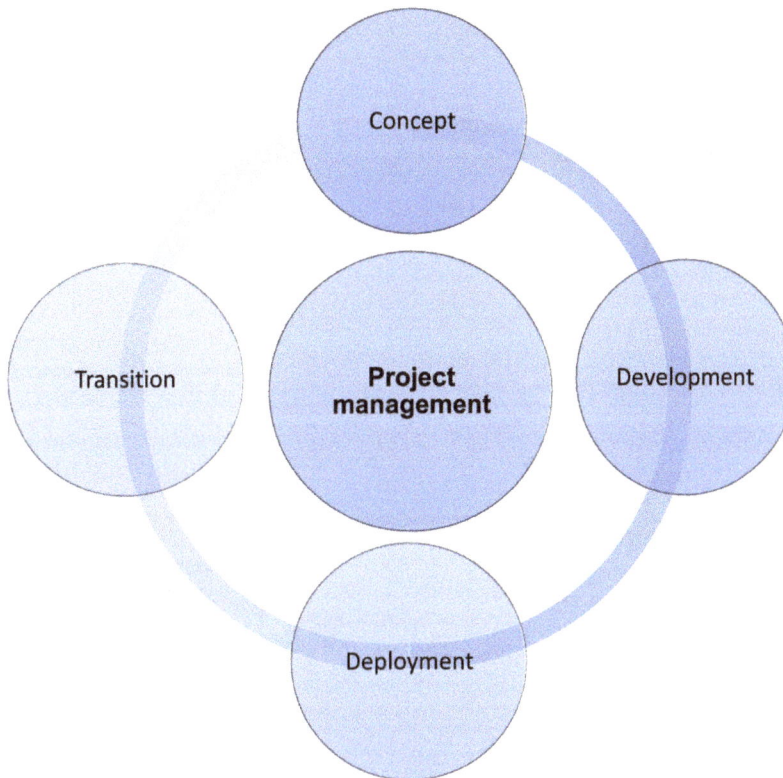

Figure 1.3 The project management process

1.6 Why should you be interested in project management?

This book is specifically written with you in mind, to guide you through these processes and methods and set you on a path to starting a whole new journey in project management or solidify your existing knowledge of project management.

Because projects are always constrained by **time, money, quality** and **risk,** the project manager must manage these constraints in such a way that the optimum balance for the project will be achieved.

An understanding of project management will help you to manage projects (your tasks/change) with confidence, ask relevant questions when involved in any project or play a key role in project delivery.

Over the years that I have been managing projects, I have come across and spoken to many **non-project managers**. I have also observed with keen interest how project management discipline is perceived by many non-project managers.

While some see project management as a **difficult, bureaucratic** and **complex discipline,** others admire project management but confess that they do not know how to get started with the basics.

> *One person said, "I would love to apply project management principles and techniques to my day-to-day work, but I don't know how; it appears to have a lot of processes, which makes it too complicated for me."*

> *Another person said, "Project management seems out of my reach. I think it is too late to get into it and apply the steps at this stage of my career."*

Maybe some of these admissions and statements resonate with you. Perhaps you have also heard of project management, read books on it and even attended courses but applying the knowledge practically is what may be lacking for you.

> *The truth is that we all apply aspects of project management principles and methods in our day-to-day lives without even realising it.*

1.7 Benefits of using project management

It has been proven over time that project management is the most effective and efficient method to manage change for the following reasons:

Table 1.3 Benefits of using project management

Common approach and understanding	Because a similar process is used, it allows everyone to use the same approach and have the same understanding. The terminologies are also very similar.
Structured approach	Just like above, project management follows step-by-step methods using life cycles to move from one stage of the project to the next.
Learning	Part of the project management process allows lessons to be captured and recorded as part of the process. This promotes constant learning from lessons.

Resource management	A good project manager will know how to utilise resources to manage projects.
Successful delivery	Project management is a specialist discipline that will equip you with the understanding and awareness of the necessary processes and methods needed to manage projects successfully and consistently.
Clearly defined roles	The roles within project management are clearly defined. This helps with good governance of projects.
Quality delivery	Project management helps to define how the project deliverables/outputs will be fit for purpose and the steps required in achieving this.
Better justification	Project management helps with establishing the reason for undertaking a project and the justification for it.
Expectation management	Project management processes allow both the client and customer to know and agree what to expect before the project is started.
Successful delivery	By adopting project management principles and methodology, it will be more likely to deliver successful projects as a result.
Efficient resource management	Project management ensures efficient and best value use of resources.
Efficient stakeholder engagement	Project management ensures effective stakeholder engagement is applied to cater for the needs and wants of the stakeholders.
Good governance	A project management methodology can be used to support the governance structure for management of a project.
Consistency	Project management offers the ability to apply a consistent approach, methodology, and process within an organisation. It is known to be one of the best approaches to ensuring consistent project delivery.

Good leadership	As a manager, director, head of department, client, etc., you may not be directly involved in the day-to-day project delivery process, but you will have a good enough understanding of projects to be able to ask the right questions or understand what is going on with projects that affect you.
	As a team member, a good understanding of project management means you can play a much more useful role in project delivery which can ultimately open doors of opportunity for you to get involved in more and bigger projects.
Business efficiency	As a business, your overall business performance partly depends on your employees' good understanding and application of project management techniques. This understanding translates into better business productivity and an efficient way of working, which also leads to a profitable business.

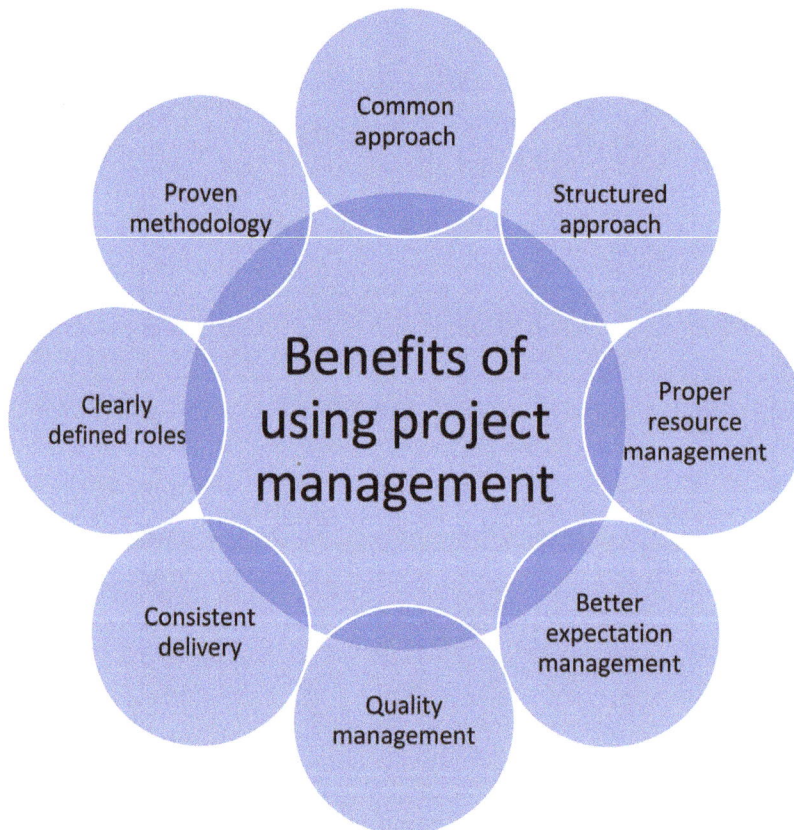

Figure 1.4 Benefits of using project management

1.8 Who is a project manager?

✓ The project manager is responsible for planning the project and ensures that it is delivered on **time** and at the agreed **cost** and **quality**.

✓ In a formal sense, a project manager is the person with the overall responsibility for managing a project through the delivery stage to handover. They help to develop the conceived idea/solution by planning how the idea will be implemented and handed over to the users.

✓ The project manager obtains information and/or coordinates input from others (designers, planners, builders, specialists, service providers, finance department, planning department, stakeholders, etc.) to help deliver the project output.

✓ The project manager is at the centre of the project and will be responsible for leading the teams, and coordinating and controlling project activities such that the desired outputs are delivered as expected, at the right cost, quality and time.

✓ They carry the title of project manager yet assume several roles during the life of the project, e.g. communicator, leader, negotiator problem-solver, go-to person, facilitator, planner, organiser, etc.

✓ The project manager develops and implements a plan for the project (project management plan).

✓ The project manager manages the project risks, issues and changes.

✓ The project manager monitors the project progress against the plan.

✓ The project manager manages the project budget.

✓ The project manager maintains communications with stakeholders and the project organisation.

✓ The project manager closes the project in a controlled manner when appropriate.

The project manager is often seen as a communicator, leader, negotiator, planner, go-to person, team builder, and many more.

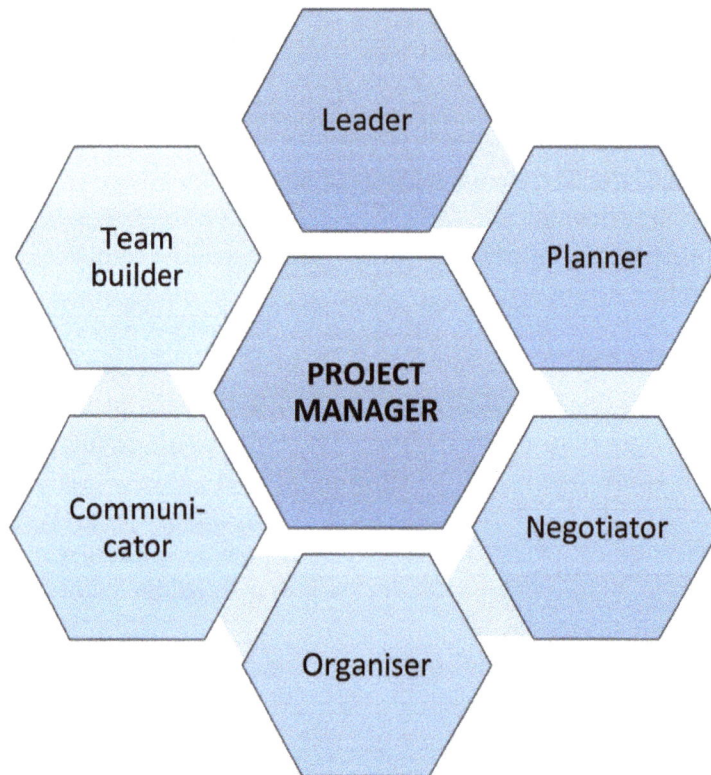

Figure 1.5 Other attributes of the project manager

1.9 Programme management

> **Programme management** is the management of a group of related projects, including business as usual activities together. A programme results in a change that is strategically beneficial to an organisation.

✓ Organisations usually have their **strategic vision** which often translates into senior leadership having to set specific objectives and targets to help realise benefits.

✓ These expected benefits will also lead to the initiation of **more than one project** at a time. Some of these individual projects may be related projects, such that together they achieve a beneficial change in line with the organisation's strategy.

✓ A programme can therefore be explained as a group of **related projects,** including **business as usual,** that together contribute to the realisation of a change that is beneficial to the organisation.

✓ Managing the **different related** projects can therefore be termed as **programme management**.

✓ For example: projects relating to car parks, long-stay car parks, short-stay car parks, car park charging, as well as the business as usual that supports these projects, can all be grouped together as a programme.

✓ Programme management is **NOT** managing more than one **unrelated** project at a time. It is also **NOT** managing a group of projects with a common resource.

✓ A programme can be put in place once the organisation determines the **strategic benefit it requires**.

✓ Programmes are not undertaken simply because it is easier to group projects together; they are first grouped and delivered together because by doing so they help the organisation's beneficial change.

1.9.1 Characteristics of programme management

✓ A programme will consist of related projects, business-as-usual and normal operations that will together provide greater benefits to the organisation when managed collectively than when managed individually.

✓ A programme will always be **dependent** upon achieving strategic benefits and the relationships the individual projects have with each other.

✓ Programme management is strategic in nature in its approach.

1.10 Portfolio management

Portfolio management is the totality of all the projects, programmes, and business as usual, an organisation can select, prioritise, and deliver to meet their overall strategic objective.

✓ Sometimes an organisation can manage programmes and projects all at the same time. When this happens, we can refer to it as a **portfolio.**

1.10.1 Characteristics of a portfolio

✓ Portfolios can be managed at an organisational or functional level.
✓ A portfolio is a selection of projects and programmes that are needed by the organisation to deliver the strategic objectives, subject to risk, resource constraints and affordability.
✓ A portfolio allows the organisation to have a view on whether the potential benefits from the organisation's investment are being realised.
✓ For an organisation to manage its portfolio effectively, it needs:
   – Strategic planning
   – To manage change effectively
   – To manage projects and programmes
✓ Portfolio management helps organisations to balance their strategic needs with changes and challenges to their operations. Portfolio management will allow decisions to start, pause, or implement new projects and programmes to be made as required, to support the organisation's strategy.

1.10.2 The benefits of applying a portfolio approach

✓ Increases the probability of realising strategic benefits which in turn make organisations valuable.
✓ Delivering projects at the portfolio level allows organisations to have a bird's eye view of risks across all their projects and programmes.
✓ As conditions continually change, organisations can apply a strategic view to all projects and programmes rather than individual projects and programmes.
✓ At a portfolio level, projects and programmes can be merged, removed, or realigned to fulfil the organisation's strategy and promote efficiency.
✓ Portfolio approach allows organisations to be efficient with how they can use and manage their resource in ever-changing times of customer demands.
✓ Resource usage is optimised at portfolio level through better allocation.

Summary

Having read this chapter, you should now be aware of and able to:

– Define the term 'project'
– Outline the project limitations
– State the differences between a project and business as usual
– Define the term 'project management'
– State the key purpose of project management
– Define the terms 'programme management' and 'portfolio management' and their relationship with project management
– State some of the reasons why a project can fail

End-of-chapter assessment

Exercise 1 – Humanitarian mission case study question

a. Using the humanitarian project identified at the start of this book, reflect and write down some of the reasons why you think this may be delivered as a project?

Exercise 2 – Humanitarian mission case study question

1   Which of the following is not a main project characteristic?

A. Projects are unique

B. Projects are large and complex

C. Projects are transient

D. Projects deliver benefits

2   Which of the following is a project not usually constrained by?

A. Cost

B. Time

C. Quality

D. People

3   Which of the following is not a benefit of using project management:

A. Helps with developing a clear roadmap for managing projects

B. Allows projects to be governed appropriately

C. Allows project lessons to be captured and learned

D. Helps individuals to cover themselves and avoid blame

4   Which of the following is not a core component of project management:

A. Decision testing

B. Defining

C. Planning

D. Monitoring

5   **Project management can be defined as:**

A. The application of processes, methods, knowledge, skills and experience to achieve the project outputs

B. The application of processes, techniques, ideas and lessons to achieve the project output

C. The process of managing a project such that the benefits are realised

D. The process of managing a project to cost, time and quality expectations.

6   **The following are all characteristics of business as usual, except:**

A. It is continuous with no end date

B. It is risk averse

C. It makes use of the benefits delivered by projects

D. It is constrained by cost, time and quality

7   **Which of the following statements best describe a programme?**

A. A group of projects managed together to deliver benefits

B. A group of related projects delivered together to deliver benefits

C. Selecting and delivering multiple related projects and business as usual in line with organisational strategy

D. A group of projects delivered under the direction of the sponsor

8   **Which of the following statements best describe a portfolio?**

A. Projects, programmes and business as usual delivered in line with an organisation's strategy

B. A selection of large and complex projects and programmes that fulfils the organisation's strategy

C. Projects and programmes that help with the realisation of the organisation's objectives

D. All of the above

9   **Which of the following is not a component of the project triangle?**

        A. Cost

        B. Time

        C. Communication

        D. Quality

10   **Which of the following can be a reason why a project can fail?**

        A. Clear project requirements

        B. Not following any plan or process

        C. Copying lessons from past and similar projects

        D. Too much stakeholder engagement

CHAPTER 2

FACTORS THAT INFLUENCE PROJECTS (PROJECT CONTEXT)

By the end of this chapter you should be able to:

– Explain why projects are affected by their environment

– Explain what is meant by the project environment/context

– Describe why PESTLE analysis might be used by a project manager

2.1 Factors that impact projects

We are in a world where many aspects of our lives are more interconnected than ever before, where one problem in a remote corner of the world can suddenly escalate to become a global problem with wider impact and implications. A seemingly simple problem in one corner of the world can suddenly escalate, impacting global economy, workforce, political decisions and many more. For example, COVID-19, popularly known as coronavirus, which started in a remote part of China, suddenly spread to become a global issue in many ways, affecting economies, transport, projects, movement of people, production, the job market and many more. It may be easy and simple to assume that projects can operate and be delivered in isolation and not be affected by things which appear remote and unrelated to that project.

As a project professional, you must be aware of all the external factors that can impact on your project, including emergence of new products, competition, innovation, new markets, etc.; these all tend to affect and add to the uncertainties around projects and their delivery.

All of these define the environment that affects projects. It can be concluded that projects do not operate in isolation; usually they are affected by the wider **environment** within which they are carried out, and even beyond. This environment is referred to as the **project context**. The project context can be internal or external to the project organisation.

For example, two projects with the same scope and requirements may be managed differently in two different environments because of the specific internal and external factors, conditions, expectations, etc. that tend to influence such projects.

Whilst one environment, e.g. the airport environment, may lay significant emphasis on security, another project environment may place its emphasis on hygiene rather than security. In the same way, a charitable project may be affected by specific factors peculiar to the charitable sector, likewise with a construction project.

In other situations, some projects may not go ahead because of the perceived impact on the environment or the perception within society. For example, the decision to build a new nuclear power station close to your community may be strongly opposed by the local community because of the perceived dangers associated with nuclear energy. Likewise, building a new airport runway may be politically motivated compared to building a new office block which may not have any political motivation. Fairly recently, the UK government's plan to extend Heathrow Airport by adding a third runway was met with significant opposition by some climate change activists. Following several years of contest, the UK government's plan for a third runway was ruled as illegal by the court of appeal on the grounds that it did not adequately take into account the government's commitment to tackle the climate crisis. This is a typical example and demonstration of a project's environmental impact and the impact that it can have on a project.

Sometimes, a small project to extend your family home could be impacted by factors such as local legislation, planning laws, opposition from neighbours, etc.

As a project professional, in addition to understanding the wider interconnectivity of your project with various external and internal factors, you can narrow these factors along the broad headings of: **political, economic, sociological, technical, legal** and **environmental** impact, simplified with the acronym **PESTLE**.

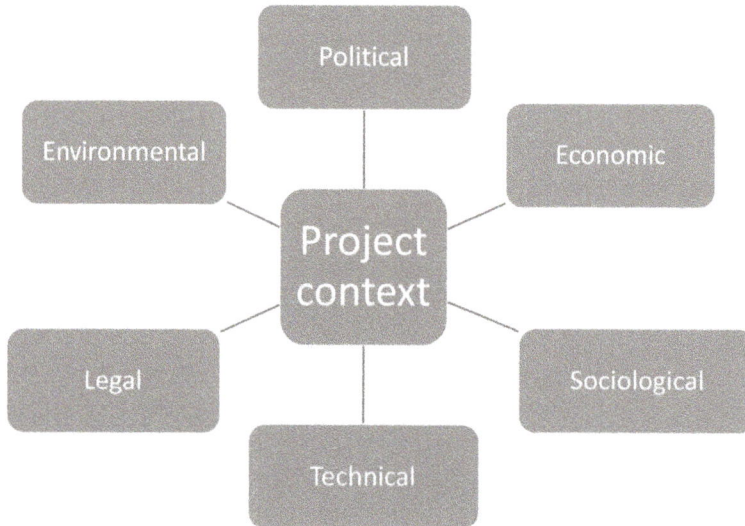

Figure 2.1 The project context

2.2 Benefits of using PESTLE analysis

Table 2.1 Benefits of using PESTLE analysis

Acronym	Meaning	Example
P	Political influence on the project	Can the political climate, both internal and external to the organisation, affect the project? For example, changes in government policies, leadership, etc.
E	Economic influence on the project	Will the current economic climate or changes to the economic climate affect the project? For example, the exchange rate or anything that can impact on money, including payment arrangements/terms.

Acronym	Meaning	Example
S	Sociological influence on the project	Social impact on the project, prevailing social order, culture, perception, etc.
T	Technical influence on the project	Is there an available technology for the project? Are there any technological challenges?
L	Legal influence on the project	Are there specific laws to be aware of? For example, regulations, legal framework, health and safety regulations, etc.
E	Environmental influence on the project	Will the project affect the environment in any way? For example, protected species, plants, deforestation, etc.

Summary

Having read this chapter you should now be aware of and able to:

– Explain why projects are affected by their environment
– Explain what is meant by the project environment/context
– Describe why PESTLE analysis might be used by a project manager

End-of-chapter assessment – factors that affect projects

Exercise 1 – Humanitarian mission project

> You have been appointed the project manager to lead this humanitarian mission.
>
> a. Your first task is to review the project context and advise your sponsor of some of the factors that could affect the success of the project.
>
> b. How will you go about identifying and analysing the project context, and what are some of the points you will raise, and why?

Exercise 2 – Humanitarian mission project

1   In project management we usually use the acronym PESTLE to analyse the project context; what does this acronym stand for?

  A. People, Economic, Society, Technological, Legal, Environment

  B. Political, Environment, Science, Training, Life cycle, Estimating

  C. Political, Economic, Sociological, Technical, Legal, Environmental

  D. Personnel, Economic, Safety, Technology, Life cycle, Estimating

2   The term 'project context' means:

  A. All the environmental factors that can affect a project

  B. The environmental changes during project delivery

  C. The environment within which the project is delivered

  D. The impact the project can have on the environment

3   A project's context should be considered on:

  A. Complex projects only

  B. Projects which are risky and selected by the sponsor

  C. Large and complex projects only

  D. All projects

4   **Which of the following is not an example of a project's context:**
   A. Changes in the political climate
   B. Availability of the right technology to support the project
   C. Perception of people in the community/society
   D. The project manager's previous experience

5   **The project environment can best be explained as:**
   A. The political impact on the project
   B. The environmental impact on the project
   C. The sociological impact on the project
   D. The environment within which a project is undertaken

6   **The project context should first be considered during:**
   A. The concept stage
   B. The planning stage
   C. The delivery stage
   D. Handover and closeout stage

7   **The project manager might use a PESTLE analysis to:**
   A. Mitigate all possible risks to the project
   B. Identify and mitigate factors that may affect the project
   C. Control technological changes during the project
   D. Consider the team social roles during the early stages of the project

8   **The following are examples of factors that impact projects:**
   A. Internal factors within the organisation
   B. Stakeholders
   C. Supply chain
   D. All of the above

CHAPTER 3

PROJECT ROLES AND RESPONSIBILITIES

By the end of this chapter you should be able to:

- Outline the roles and responsibilities of the project sponsor
- Outline the roles and responsibilities of the project manager
- Outline the roles and responsibilities of the following: project governance, project team members, end users, product owner and the project management office

3.1 The project sponsor

You may have heard the term 'sponsorship' time and time again. Depending on how you look at it, sponsorship could mean committing money or resources, for example, to an event or to make something happen. For example, your organisation may agree to sponsor an upcoming event, a programme or even a person to complete, for example, their education.

Whilst all of these are correct with the general sponsorship terminology, 'sponsorship' in project management means something slightly different. A sponsor in project management is an active role performed by a **named person.**

The following are some of the roles expected to be fulfilled by the sponsor, sometimes referred to as the **project executive, project director, senior responsible owner, project champion**, etc.:

✓ The sponsor is usually senior to the project manager and assists the project manager to manage key stakeholders.
✓ Should be quite senior within the organisation, at least should be senior to the project manager. Must be able to have influence, with the ability to work and relate with other business leaders and facilitate decision making or make key decisions.
✓ Initiates the project and ensures a project manager is appointed.
✓ Produces and owns the overall **business case** (must justify why the project should be undertaken).
✓ Is responsible for making sure the project benefits are realised.
✓ Should be a different person from the project manager.
✓ Helps to define the project's success criteria.
✓ Monitors the project and makes controlled decisions.
✓ Approves the project communication management plan.
✓ Ensures the project is governed effectively.
✓ Ensures the project is properly closed out.
✓ Ensures relevant authorities are in place to approve the project to progress.

Figure 3.1 Roles of the project sponsor

3.2 The project manager

✓ Is responsible for managing the project at hand and ensures that it is delivered on time and within budget.

✓ Manages the project resource and scope to ensure that the project is delivered as promised.

✓ Oversees the day-to-day running of the project.

✓ Ensures the work is done to the right quality.

✓ Coordinates with different people for the work to be done.

✓ Deals with changes that occur on the project.

✓ Manages the expectations of the sponsor and the stakeholders.

✓ Makes decisions in a timely manner to ensure the project succeeds.

✓ Plans what work needs to be done, when and by whom.

✓ Monitors and manages the project risks and escalates issues where required.

✓ Communicates with the stakeholders.

✓ Acts as the main point of contact with the team members, other organisations, contractors and suppliers.

✓ Monitors and controls the project progress.

✓ Builds, leads and motivates the project team throughout the project delivery.

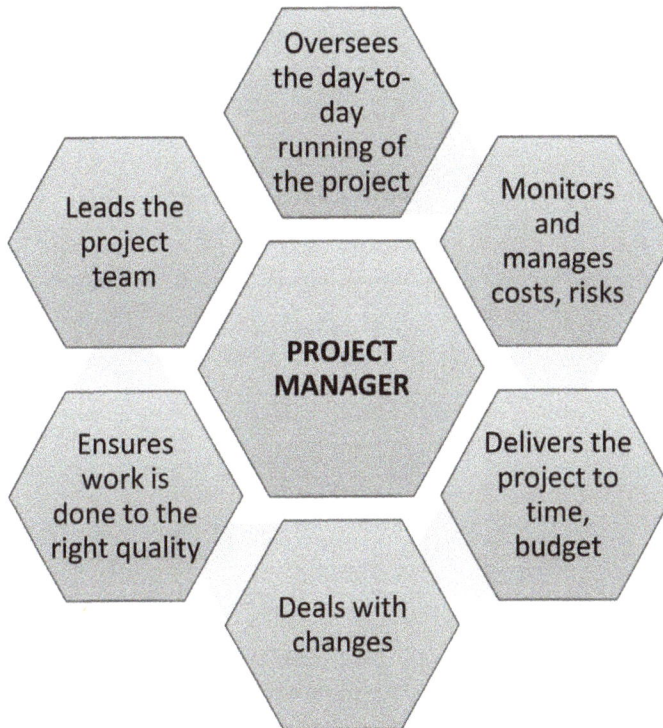

Figure 3.2 Roles of the project manager

3.3 The team leader

✓ Is responsible for the team's work and in most organisations is the first level of management to whom the team reports.
✓ Has the responsibility of coaching, coordinating, solving problems, sharing information, reporting status, liaising with higher management or administration, etc.
✓ Usually splits their time between management and technical/functional responsibilities.

3.4 The project governance

✓ Project governance ensures that the right conditions/environment are created to make it necessary for the project to be delivered efficiently. Governance allows projects with the chance to be delivered successfully.
✓ Projects which lack proper governance often cannot provide the right assurance to the stakeholders and those who matter.
✓ Lack of proper governance derails confidence in the project.

✓ Project governance ensures that the right controls, measures and processes are in place to support successful project delivery.

✓ Governance ensures there are basic strategies in place to ensure the project benefits can and will be realised.

✓ Proper project governance supports project justification and subsequent approval of the business case.

✓ There are several ways that effective project governance can be established, including establishing clear roles and responsibilities using the responsibility assignment matrix.

✓ Proper project governance is key to ensuring projects progress through the relevant life cycle phases by meeting the minimum expectations.

✓ Proper project governance can be used as a tool to provide effective feedback and information to key project stakeholders and the project sponsor.

3.5 The project team members

✓ The group of people who have come together to collaborate for the purpose of cooperating towards the project implementation.

✓ The team members are responsible for implementing the relevant tasks as assigned by the project manager.

✓ Team members are required to work together to complement each other with their skills.

✓ The project team is responsible for managing and delivering all the technical requirements that will deliver the project.

3.6 The project end users

✓ Individuals, groups, teams, organisations, that will become the beneficiaries or users of the completed project.

✓ Users can also be the person, or group of people or organisation, who is intended to benefit from the project.

✓ Users specify the operational requirements.

✓ They accept and operate the deliverable to achieve the defined benefits.

✓ They separate the project 'musts' and 'wants'.

✓ They help identify the project constraints.

✓ They assist the project manager with the project handover and acceptance.

✓ They inform the project manager of operational changes and issues.

✓ They are an integral part of the project team.

3.7 The product owner

✓ A product owner can be the main representative on behalf of an organisation or the user community. The product owner will be responsible for working with the user group to determine the features of the product.
✓ A product owner is the link between the customers and the product development team.
✓ The product owner manages ambiguities and ensures there is clear understanding of product requirements between the users and the development team.
✓ The product owner ensures the organisation derives the maximum benefit and value from the product.

3.8 The project management office (PMO)

✓ The project management office is a group internal or external to the organisation.
✓ It sets, maintains and ensures standards for project management across the organisation are consistent.
✓ The project office usually takes some of the administrative burden off the project manager.
✓ It can be the **custodian** of standards, documents and templates and ensure they are all up to date.

3.9 The project stakeholders

✓ Every project, regardless of size, will have a positive or negative impact on another person, team, business, group, etc.
✓ For a project to be delivered successfully, the relevant stakeholders must be identified, analysed and engaged.
✓ Stakeholders can influence the outcome of every project.
✓ Stakeholders can provide useful insight into projects.

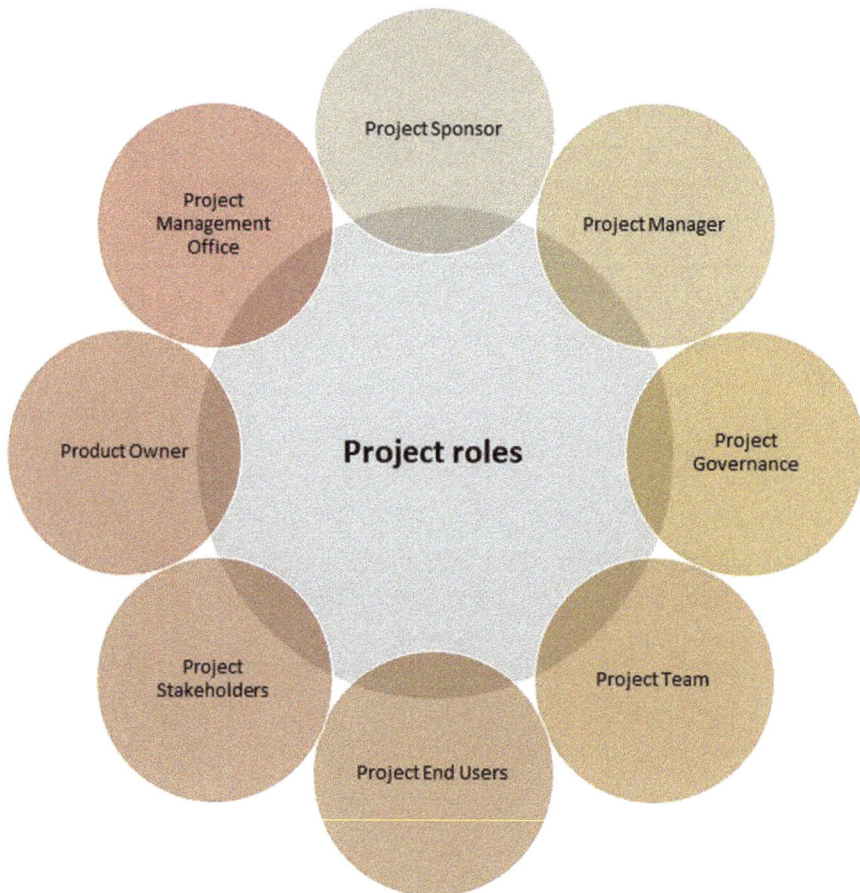

Figure 3.3 Some roles in project delivery

Summary

Having read this chapter you should now be aware of and able to:

- Outline the roles and responsibilities of the project sponsor
- Outline the roles and responsibilities of the project manager
- Outline the roles and responsibilities of the following: project governance, project team members, end users, product owner and the project management office

End-of-chapter assessment – project roles and responsibilities

Exercise 1 – Humanitarian mission project

As the project sponsor, you want to assemble a team to assist with the project delivery. Identity the key roles you will require and bullet point the high-level duties you will expect each role to play.

Exercise 2 – Humanitarian mission project

1 The day-to-day management of the project is the responsibility of?

A. The project manager

B. The project sponsor

C. The project team

D. All of the above

2 Who will usually initiate a project and ensure the benefits are documented and realised?

A. The project manager

B. The project sponsor

C. The project director

D. Whoever is the leader of the organisation

3 The role of the project manager and the project sponsor can be performed by the same person to minimise costs.

A. True

B. False

4　In some organisations where there is a project management office, which one will not be a typical duty?

A. Guide the project manager

B. Take some of the admin duties from the project manager

C. Maintain standards for the whole organisation

D. Act as custodians of standards and documents

5　Which of the following is not a benefit of project governance:

A. Ensures the right environment and conditions for the project to perform are created

B. Promotes confidence that the project is progressing as expected

C. Ensures the project progresses through the life cycles

D. Ensures the project manager is effectively monitored

6　Which of the following may not be a typical role performed by the project end users:

A. They make use of the project benefits

B. They help to clarify the project requirements

C. They define the operational requirements

D. They approve the project management plan

7　Which of the following is not true about stakeholders:

A. Influence the project outcome

B. Provide useful insight into the project

C. Help the project manager

D. Appoint a project manager

8　Who is the person responsible for acting as the liaison between the users and the product development team?

A. Product manager

B. Project manager

C. Product owner

D. Project sponsor

9   The group of individuals who come together to collaborate for the purpose of achieving the project objectives is the:

A. Project stakeholders

B. Project team

C. Project management office

D. Project users

10   Who will typically put the project team together?

A. Project manager

B. Project sponsor

C. Project stakeholders

D. Project executive

CHAPTER 4

UNDERSTANDING THE PROJECT LIFE CYCLES

By the end of this chapter you should be able to:

- State the phases of a typical linear project life cycle
- State the phases of a typical iterative project life cycle
- Define the term 'hybrid life cycle'
- Define the term 'extended project life cycle'

4.1 Project life cycle

> **A project life cycle** represents the distinct stages of a project. It is used to provide a structure for undertaking the project and governing it effectively.

You must have heard this metaphorical question before: **"How do you eat an elephant?"** While it may seem an impossible undertaking, this is intended to imply that **you can tackle anything one bite at a time.**

Projects are metaphorically like eating an elephant. Regardless of their value, size and complexity, they can also be broken down and tackled one bite at a time.

In project management, these strategic bites are what are called PROJECT STAGES/ PHASES. The complete process involving all the stages/phases from start to finish is the **PROJECT LIFE CYCLE.**

The life cycle is useful for creating a clearly laid down roadmap for breaking down the project delivery into various manageable chunks. Life cycle can be seen as phases of project activities delivered in sequence. The project life cycle provides a good structure that allows projects to be delivered in gradual steps.

Several approaches have been developed for delivering projects through a life cycle. These approaches range from **predictive**, where activities within each life cycle stage are fully defined, to **adaptive**, where the activities within the life cycle stage keep changing, allowing learning and understanding as the project develops.

A house-building project can follow a predictive life cycle approach because the full project detail (scope and requirements) can easily be determined, planned and predicted.

Conversely, creating a bespoke product, like new computer software to track employee well-being, may require a series of iterations before the full and detailed requirements can be understood and developed.

There is never a singularly perfect life cycle suitable for all projects. Sometimes predictive or adaptive on their own may not be useful and beneficial to deliver a project. This has led to the creation of another type of life cycle approach that combines the benefits of both the predictive and adaptive approaches to form a **hybrid life cycle** approach. In a hybrid approach, the initial development goes through iterations to a point where the requirement and scope are fully understood, followed by a predictive approach to completion. Such a life cycle, that merges the benefit of both an iterative and predictive approach, may be called a hybrid life cycle.

4.2 The linear project life cycle (short life cycle)

A linear life cycle typically has the following phases

–   Concept (initiation, development)
–   Definition (detailed definition, planning)
–   Deployment (delivery/implementation/execution)
–   Transition (handover, closeout)

> **A LINEAR project life cycle** is associated with projects that are delivered by following a straight and unidirectional sequence. For example, from the initial concept through to implementation and handover of the project.

✓   Project work, regardless of size, can follow the **linear life cycle** process for delivering the project idea into outputs/outcomes.
✓   A linear project life cycle is useful for projects where the project activities, requirements and scope are fully understood and can easily be defined.

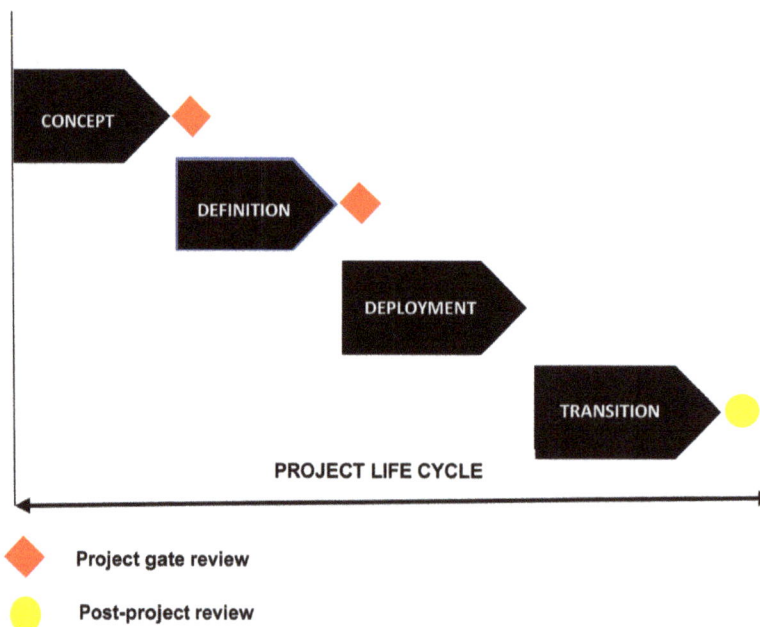

Figure 4.1 The linear project life cycle stages

✓ For example, the **humanitarian project** used as our case study in this book can be delivered using a linear life cycle. If the output, requirement and scope for each phase of the project can be well defined, this allows the project to be completed sequentially with a high degree of certainty.

✓ Each completed phase represents a partially completed overall project.

4.2.1 Characteristics of a linear life cycle

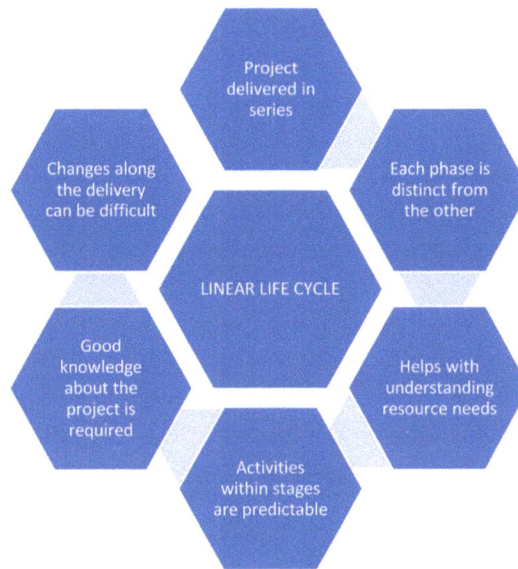

Figure 4.2 Characteristics of a linear project life cycle

4.3 The iterative project life cycle (adaptive life cycle)

Iteration simply means repeating a process in order to generate a sequence of outcomes. The iterative life cycle comes from the idea of **iterations**, where a phase of the project can undergo several **iterations** until we are certain of the outcomes, expectations, requirements and scope, etc. before progressing to the next phase.

> **An ITERATIVE project life cycle** makes allowance for some of the project stages to be repeated severally to get right prior to progressing to the subsequent stages. This allows better understanding of the project objective and scope.

An iterative life cycle is different from a linear life cycle because the iterative allows the project team to go back and forth and make changes within a stage until it is certain to progress to the next stage in the project life cycle. A linear life cycle, on the other hand, is a single pass through the life cycle, with very little room to go back and forth, especially when the scope has been frozen. Changes can be allowed but may be costly, especially if made after the change freeze.

An example of a project that can use iteration is the development of a new software application. Uncertainties and lack of clarity with requirement, scope and expected performance in practice may lead to the project work being developed through several iterations.

A prototype may be developed, rolled out and tested for feedback. This process can be repeated several times until the requirements and scope are clear and well understood before progressing to next life cycle phase.

The iterative life cycle is more fluid and the detail is refined as the project develops and lessons are learned. **Agile** project management is based on this type of idea.

Sometimes, to prevent back and forth changes from going on forever resulting in a protracted project delivery, the idea of **timeboxing** can be used. A **timebox** is where the overall duration is set for a process. For example, the concept stage of an iterative life cycle can be timeboxed to complete within, say, three months from the start date.

This timebox idea then controls the project time and allows it to move along to achieve the target date without delay while at the same time progressing on the principle of iteration.

4.3.1 Characteristics of the iterative life cycle

✓ You know what you want (goal) but how to get it is not fully known
✓ Flexible in developing several iterations until you are sure before proceeding
✓ Changes are expected as the project progresses
✓ Lessons are learned and used to improve the product as it develops
✓ It is useful for addressing innovative, pioneering changes which are untested
✓ The scope grows and becomes more understood as the project develops
✓ Project requirements allowed to develop as the project progresses
✓ Timeboxing is usually applied to control/manage completion time
✓ It becomes useful when feedback on iterations are obtained to improve products or revise requirements

4.4 The iterative life cycle phases

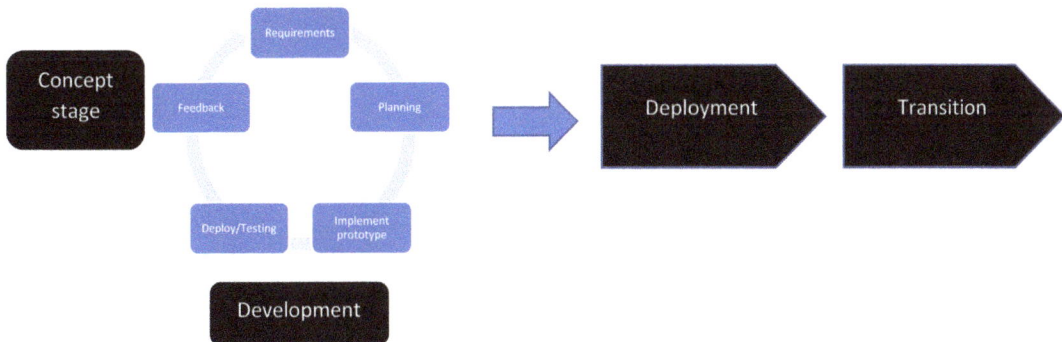

Figure 4.3 The iterative project life cycle stages

4.5 The hybrid project life cycle

> **A hybrid life cycle** – the approach combines the benefits of both the linear and iterative life cycles to create this new life cycle

The hybrid life cycle makes use of both the **linear** and **iterative** life cycles to create a new life cycle which is a hybrid of the two cycles. The expectation is that the hybrid life cycle will take advantage of the iterative cycle to develop one phase of the hybrid life cycle, for example the development stage.

This allows the requirement and scope to be fully developed as they go through several iterations. It also allows the project to enter the deployment stage with a high degree of certainty and understanding. The likelihood of success through the deployment stage is very high for a hybrid life cycle.

The hybrid life cycle is beneficial for gaining a good understanding of the project prior to progressing to subsequent stages.

4.5.1 Characteristics of the hybrid life cycle

- ✓ Combines iterative and linear
- ✓ Initial development stage can be iterative followed by linear
- ✓ Allows a more robust delivery stage if the development stages are based on an iterative approach

4.6 The extended project life cycle (long life cycle)

Projects do not always end after handover and closeout. Usually the handover phase marks the beginning of a new phase of incorporating the project output into business as usual. This phase also commences the process of realising the benefits as outlined in the project justification. Some projects will also have a life span over which the deliverables are expected to last before disposal.

Sometimes projects can be planned, delivered, operated and disposed of all as one project life cycle approach. This is another kind of life cycle called the **extended life cycle**. Extended life cycles do not just happen by bolting on to the end of the project operation and subsequent disposal. To deliver a project using the extended life cycle route requires a series of planning and decision-making upfront, from the concept stage and throughout the project.

Early decisions have to be made to incorporate into the project requirements how the outputs will be operated and the benefits realised.

Certain decisions have to be made about disposal at the early stages of the project and throughout planning. Perhaps the need for disposal by a certain date will affect what the project is and how it is planned.

An extended project life cycle ensures that the project benefits realisation are embedded within the organisation.

An EXTENDED life cycle is like any standard life cycle (linear, iterative) that extends to include additional phases of adopting the project into business as usual to realise the project benefits and through to disposal.

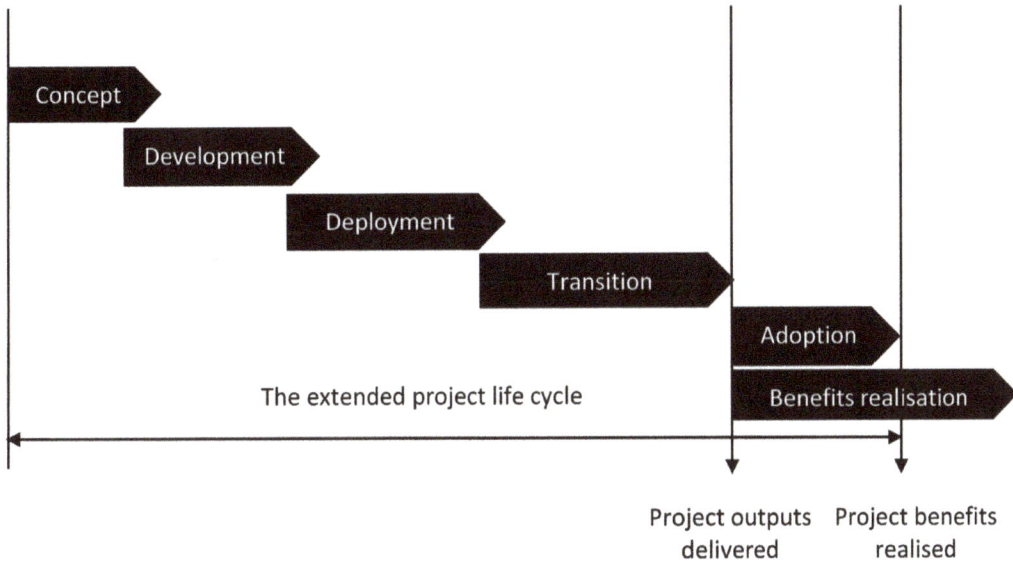

Figure 4.4 The extended project life cycle stages

4.7 Concept (initiation) phase

Can you recollect a time when you thought of a wonderful idea only to realise after careful consideration that it was not an idea worth pursuing? Perhaps, after careful consideration, you found the planned solution or approach to be too risky, costly or impractical. Maybe you found out that spending time, effort and money to pursue the idea would not yield the expected benefits.

Such consideration is exactly what goes into investigating and assessing a project idea at the **concept stage**. The fact that a project idea is brought up does not mean it is worth pursuing. The idea must be carefully thought through and evaluated to make an informed decision as to whether it is worth investing time and effort in it.

The conclusion of the concept or initiation stage of the project will be marked with a decision by the project sponsor or the organisation to progress the project to the second stage (development stage).

Generally, the concept stage is where the **problem or opportunity** that will give rise to the project is clearly defined. You may spend some time to conduct a **study into the viability** of the **need** and the preferred solution.

4.7.1 What you may consider at the concept stage

✓ Know what the actual need or problem is
✓ Know the main benefits you expect

✓ Write your high-level requirements (wants and needs)
✓ Review your requirements
✓ Consider alternative options you can use to achieve the required benefits
✓ Consider each option and think about the associated risks
✓ Carry out a financial check on each option, e.g. return on investment, discounted rate of return, etc., and decide if it is worth investing money in the project
✓ Estimate how much each option may cost
✓ Estimate how long each option may take to complete
✓ Select a preferred option
✓ A business case is usually developed to conclude the findings of the concept stage. This document is also used to obtain approval from management, funders, project owners, etc. to progress the project to the next stage.
✓ Ensure a firm reason or rationale for the project is established and documented
✓ Identify at this early stage the key stakeholders
✓ The concept stage is useful for finding stakeholders and analysing stakeholders
✓ Seek advice, if necessary, from senior managers

4.8 Development (planning/definition) stage

The development stage is where the **preferred option** is carefully planned.

Failing to plan a project properly will ultimately lead to problems or difficulties with cost/time overruns, quality issues, uncontrolled scope changes, etc.

During project planning, the first important document the project manager **begins** to prepare is the **project management plan (PMP).** The PMP is finalised as an output of the planning stage. It clarifies and explains how the project manager plans to manage the project at hand. In summary, the PMP will address the what, when, who, how, where, etc. of the project.

Once completed, the PMP must be **shared with the key stakeholders** so they are fully aware of what the project is and how it will be delivered.

The PMP will usually address the following:

- **Scope** – what exactly will be delivered and not delivered
- **Risks** – how will they be managed
- **Quality** – how this will be achieved, monitored, etc.
- **Success** – how this will be measured and with what
- **Stakeholders** – how they will be identified and managed
- **Resources** – how you will find and fund these for the project
- **Changes** – how they will be managed when they happen

The PMP is an **active** document which must be kept up to date (updated when new information becomes available) during the life of the project.

Whether a project is small or large, simple or complicated, planning is an essential activity. It provides clarity on how the project will be delivered using the available budget, within the expected timeframe and with existing constraints.

The planning stage could be much simpler and shorter, taking a few hours or days to complete. It all depends on the size and complexity of the project at hand.

4.9 Considerations at the development phase

✓ Refine the project scope.
✓ Refine the project requirements
✓ Analyse and engage stakeholders
✓ Plan the project quality expectations
✓ Define the project roles and responsibilities
✓ Plan how risks will be managed
✓ Plan how project changes and issues will be managed
✓ Produce a Project Management Plan (PMP). Some organisations refer to it as a Project Initiation Document (PID) or Project Execution Plan (PEP).

4.10 Deployment (delivery/implementation/execution) phase

The project manager overseeing the project delivery has the responsibility to ensure that all planned activities required for a successful delivery are carried out in the sequential/concurrent order as planned.

The project manager will be at the centre of the delivery process: **coordinating, controlling, managing teams, communicating, planning, monitoring, providing resources, engaging and updating stakeholders,** etc.

Being vigilant at this stage of the project is essential for the success of the project.

4.11 Monitoring and controlling the project

The monitoring stage of the project happens concurrently with the delivery. Monitoring means keeping a watchful eye on the project and steering it in the right direction.

The project manager keeps an eye on the project by ensuring that everything is happening as planned and changes are controlled. Some of the things the project manager monitors are:

-   **Scope** – any change to the agreed scope must be captured, recorded and assessed
-   **Risks** – are responded to appropriately
-   **Quality** – is monitored through inspection, testing, questioning, etc.
-   **Budget vs spend** – how the project is spending compared to your budget
-   **Programme** – are you on target to finish on time?
-   **Implement** what has been planned
-   **Monitor and control** the project schedule and carry out reviews to ensure the project is on the right track
-   **Comms** – implement stakeholder communication plans
-   **Leadership** – exercise good leadership and support the team

Be clear early on in the project what will be monitored, how it will be monitored and the frequency.

Keep accurate **records** of your project information, not only for audit purposes but to ensure you have the documents which will enable you to monitor changes.

4.12 Transition (handover and closeout) phase

This represents the last stage of the linear/iterative/hybrid (except extended) project life cycle. At this stage, all the work will have been completed and the project manager is able to hand over the project to the customer for **beneficial use**.

It is common for a project to be completed and handed over for beneficial use yet fall into the trap of not properly handing over all the important documentation required.

At the handover stage, several activities may be required, including: demonstration, training, testing, etc. to confirm conformance to an agreed standard or quality expectation, legislation, etc.

The customer must accept all relevant documentation and sign it off to officially accept the project as meeting the **success criteria**.

4.12.1 Consideration during handover and closeout

-   ✓ Invite stakeholders to a handover meeting/demonstration where applicable
-   ✓ Check whether you have delivered the original project objectives and requirements and you have not gone out of scope
-   ✓ Prepare handover notes where applicable
-   ✓ Arrange sign-off in line with the agreed project acceptance criteria
-   ✓ Issue completion certificate, test certificate, operating manuals, etc.
-   ✓ Organise training where required
-   ✓ Capture and record project lessons
-   ✓ Disband team and clear site

✓ Make sure you have delivered against budget, quality requirements and the end deadline
✓ Understand how well you managed risks and your key stakeholders – use questionnaires to obtain feedback
✓ Prepare a list of unfinished items, identify who will complete these after the project and circulate to any stakeholders

4.13 Reasons for splitting projects into phases

The project life cycle is a good way to demonstrate or communicate how a project will progress over time.

Each life cycle stage has clearly defined activities and outputs.

The end of each life cycle stage represents an opportunity for the project team and the sponsor to take a break and review the project: whether to progress or stop (**gate review**).

Each stage in the life cycle requires a different level and amount of resource. This means the life cycle stages help us to understand the resources needed to complete the project.

A project life cycle consists of several distinct phases. **Life cycle stages break down a project into manageable pieces.**

Summary

Having read this chapter you should now be aware of and able to:

– State the phases of a typical linear project life cycle
– State the phases of a typical iterative project life cycle
– Define the term 'hybrid life cycle'
– Define the term 'extended project life cycle'

End-of-chapter assessment – project life cycle

Exercise 1 – Humanitarian mission project

a. Using the humanitarian mission project identified at the start of this book, split this project into relevant delivery phases.

b. In bullet points, identify some of the main activities you will carry out within each of the phases/stages.

Exercise 2 – Humanitarian mission project

1   **The linear project life cycle phases are in this order:**

A. Concept, Planning, Definition, Handover, Closeout

B. Explore, Concept, Definition, Planning, Handover

C. Concept, Definition, Deployment, Transition

D. None of the above

2   **The project life cycle can be defined as the:**

A. Interrelated phases of a project that provide the structure for governing the progression of the work

B. The division of the project into smaller pieces for easy delivery

C. The cycle a project must go through to avoid missing anything

D. The stages some organisations have chosen to manage their projects

3   **Which of the following is not a reason to structure projects into phases?**

A. Helps to communicate clearly how the project will progress over time

B. Allows the sponsor and the management an opportunity to take a break at the end of each phase to decide whether to progress or not

C. Helps to understand the resources needed for each stage

D. All of the above

4   **Which of the following is not an activity during the handover and closeout stage of a project?**

A. Handover notes are prepared

B. Lessons learned are captured and recorded

C. Project benefits are identified

D. Training is organised for the users where applicable

5   **Which of the following is not a project development stage activity?**

A. The project management plan is prepared

B. A detailed risk assessment is carried out

C. A detailed stakeholder assessment is carried out

D. All changes are frozen

6   **At what point during the project delivery will the project benefits and justification be documented?**

A. Concept stage

B. Planning stage

C. Definition stage

D. All of the above

7   **The business case is the output of the:**

A. Concept stage

B. Definition stage

C. Implementation stage

D. Handover/closeout stage

8   **One key benefit of using an extended project life cycle is to:**

A. Extend the project delivery when time is limited

B. Extend the project life cycle to ensure quality delivery

C. Ensure the benefit realisation stays with the change team

D. Ensure the project benefits can be extended for years to come

9   **Which project life cycle would be suitable for a project with unclear scope and objective:**

A. Linear project life cycle

B. Hybrid project life cycle

C. Iterative project life cycle

D. Extended project life cycle

10   **A hybrid life cycle will usually make use of both the:**

A. Linear and extended project life cycle

B. Hybrid and linear project life cycle

C. Iterative and linear project life cycle

D. All of the above

CHAPTER 5

ESTABLISHING THE PROJECT NEED (THE WHY)

By the end of this chapter you should be able to:

- Outline the importance of establishing the project need

- Define the term 'benefit management'

- Distinguish between different types of benefits

- Identify and group project benefits

- Explain SMART project benefits

5.1 Project benefits

> **Benefits** are 'positive and measurable impact resulting from the delivery of a project' - (Murray-Webster, Dalcher and Association for Project Management, 2019).

You should already be aware that projects are carried out to deliver outputs which should ultimately lead to **benefits**. This means there cannot be a project without an **associated benefit.**

It is also common for projects to be undertaken without properly understanding or agreeing the full benefits. This often leads to difficulties when measuring the benefits after project completion, thus making it even more difficult to tell whether the project was successful or not.

The identification of project benefits and documenting them is the responsibility of the project sponsor (project executive/senior responsible owner). It can also be the person for whom the project is being delivered.

When documenting project benefits, it will not be enough to only state the expected project benefits and expect that they will be realised. To realise project benefits may require the expense of **time, effort** and **money**. For this reason, a potential project benefit can sometimes be discounted because the associated time, effort and money required to realise the benefit far outweighs the benefit expected.

For example, if it may cost you 20% more to purchase a car with satellite navigation, you could weigh up this cost against the benefit you will get from having a car with such a functionality. Some benefits are very valuable such that they far outweigh the cost, effort and time input, for example benefits relating to health, safety and welfare.

Project benefits can be analysed with a SMART criterion to determine how Specific, Measurable, Attainable and Relevant they are.

5.2 Understanding SMART benefits

Table 5.1 SMART project benefits

Specific	The project benefits should be detailed and clear and must ideally answer the questions, **why, what, how, who** and **when**, of the project. Example: increase the capacity from 20 parking spaces to 50, increase the size of the existing building by 20%, increase attendance by 50% from the previous year. These are more specific than stating 'increase attendance from the previous year as an example.

Measurable	You should be able to tell/measure when you get to the benefit or achieve it. This means you should be able to find the answers to the when, how, who, why, etc. of the project.
	Example: the increase in car parking spaces can be measured immediately after the project, increasing the size of the existing building can be measured after the project, and the same with increasing an event attendance by 50%.
	A benefit, like using sustainable materials on your project to reduce global warming, cannot be easily measured.
Achievable	Ensure the benefits can be achieved.
	Some benefits are clearly not achievable. Using the benefits above, if there is no land capacity to increase the car parking spaces from 20 to 50, then that benefit cannot be achieved.
	The same applies to expanding the existing building size and the event attendance. By deciding to increase the event attendance by 50%, there should be the logistics to cater for the increase.
Relevant	Some benefits may not be relevant or necessary, so make sure your project benefits are relevant.
	You want to increase the car parking spaces, however you want to use asphalt instead of just gravel in an area where gravel is ideal.
	You want to increase the building capacity by 50% but you want the extension to be built with stones and marble compared to the existing building which is built with timber. Unless there is a good reason for it, building the extension with marble and stone may not be relevant.
Time related	The benefits should be achievable in the available time period. This should be as detailed as possible and not a vague estimation. Can the additional car parking spaces be delivered within the timeframe expected? Can the event be organised with increased attendance within the timeframe expected?

5.3 Understanding some benefit categories

Table 5.2 Project benefit categories

Benefits can further be categorised into:

Direct benefits	Examples – increase in capacity, size, amount Examples – increase car parking spaces, increase attendance by 50%, etc.
Indirect non-financial benefits	Examples – improved morale, satisfaction

Indirect financial benefits	Examples – discounts, freebies. 50% off all hotel booking between January and March. Staff can book car parking spaces at 25% discount.
Intangible benefits	Examples – increase in loyal customers, brand awareness

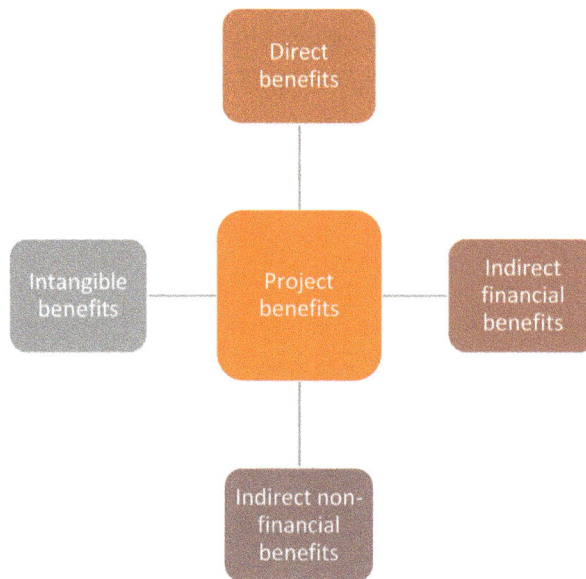

Figure 5.1 Project benefit categories

Benefits management is 'the identification, definition, planning, tracking and realisation of benefits' - (Murray-Webster, Dalcher and Association for Project Management, 2019).

Summary

Having read this chapter you should now be aware of and able to:

- Outline the importance of establishing the project need
- Define the term 'benefit management'
- Distinguish between different types of benefits
- Identify and group project benefits
- Explain SMART project benefits

End-of-chapter assessment – project benefits

Exercise 1 – Humanitarian mission project

> Using the **humanitarian mission project,** the project directors have written the main project benefits for inclusion in the business case. You are not convinced that you can measure these benefits as they do not seem real. Write what you think should be the main project benefits and categorise these to demonstrate to your manager how these benefits can be measured.

---

1 **All project benefits can easily be measured.**
   A. True
   B. False

2 **All projects must deliver outputs which should lead to benefits.**
   A. True
   B. False

3 **Project benefits can be explained as:**
   A. Potential improvement as a result of project outputs
   B. The main deliverables that make the customer happy
   C. The improvement that results from the completion of a project
   D. The measurable improvement that results from the completion of a project

4 **It is possible for some project benefits to be negative.**
   A. True
   B. False

5   As part of employment package, new staff are entitled to a 20% discount
        on all IT products. This is an example of:
        A. Direct non-financial benefit
        B. Indirect financial benefit
        C. Indirect benefit
        D. Intangible benefit

6   Which of these is true about intangible benefits?
        A. Can be measured but over a very long period
        B. Can be difficult to measure
        C. Can only be measured by the project manager
        D. Increasing cash is an example

CHAPTER 6

ENGAGING THE PROJECT STAKEHOLDERS

By the end of this chapter you should be able to:

- Explain who stakeholders are
- State some of the techniques for identifying stakeholders
- Sketch a simple stakeholder grid to demonstrate power and interest
- Explain the meaning of a 'stakeholder management plan'
- Explain why communicating with stakeholders is important

6.1 Project stakeholders

Projects by their nature usually attract attention from people, groups or organisations in one way or another. This attention may generate **support, opposition** or an **interest** in the project.

> **Stakeholders** are individuals, teams, groups, or an organisation that may be interested, affected, or play a role in the project.

The step-by-step process of **identifying, analysing, planning** and **implementing** actions designed to engage with stakeholders is called **stakeholder management.**

The statement above means that all stakeholders should be **proactively identified**, their **interest** and **influence** analysed, and subsequently engaged such that they do not negatively affect the project objectives.

Every project, regardless of size, complexity or value, will have stakeholders who may need to be **influenced, kept informed, updated** and **engaged.**

Stakeholder support should be maintained throughout the project delivery to guarantee project success. Stakeholders are important for every project because they can provide **useful ideas, insight** and **information** to shape how the project is delivered. They can also oppose, reject and negatively influence the project.

Managing stakeholders is a **proactive process** of **identifying, analysing** and **engaging** with a view to meeting stakeholders' needs and wants, and reaching a compromise, win-win solution or influencing them.

The project manager must develop a plan and put a strategy in place to **identify, analyse** *and* **influence** stakeholders throughout the project delivery.

The following explains the steps involved in stakeholder engagement:

1. Stakeholder identification
2. Stakeholder analysis
3. Stakeholder engagement

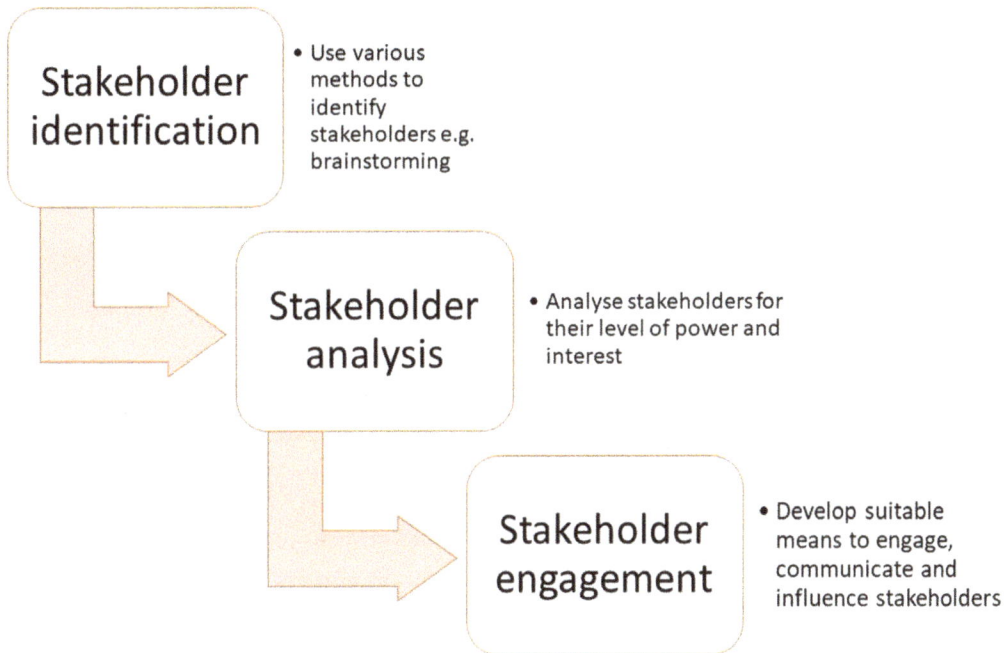

Figure 6.1 Stakeholder engagement steps

6.2 How to identify the project stakeholders

It is important to know that **not** all stakeholders will be **obvious** to the project manager and the team from the start of the project. Usually a proactive effort is required to identify stakeholders who might otherwise not readily come to mind. Missing out stakeholders can have a detrimental impact on the project.

For example, stakeholders can hold vital project information or provide early project support. To avoid missing key stakeholders, it is good practice to involve other team members, experts and the use of various techniques to help identify stakeholders.

Techniques like brainstorming sessions, checklists, past knowledge, lessons from previous projects, etc. help to identify potential individuals, teams or organisations that may be potential stakeholders.

Examples of potential stakeholders

– The sponsor	– Retailers
– End users	– Police
– Interest groups	– Emergency services
– Disability groups	– Car park operations
– Trades unions	– Cleaning firms
– Customers	– Security
– Residents	– Taxi operatives
– Local government	– Shop owners
– Subject matter experts	– Parents

6.3 How to analyse stakeholders

Stakeholder analysis involves the grouping of stakeholders according to the level of **POWER/INFLUENCE** and **INTEREST** they have or are perceived to have on the project.

The result of stakeholder analysis is the creation of the **STAKEHOLDER IMPACT GRID**. This is a commonly used tool for grouping stakeholders according to their level of power, influence and interest in the project.

There are other ways to represent stakeholder analysis; however, the basic technique is the use of the **stakeholder impact grid**. This provides a powerful visual aid that helps to see stakeholder impact at a glance.

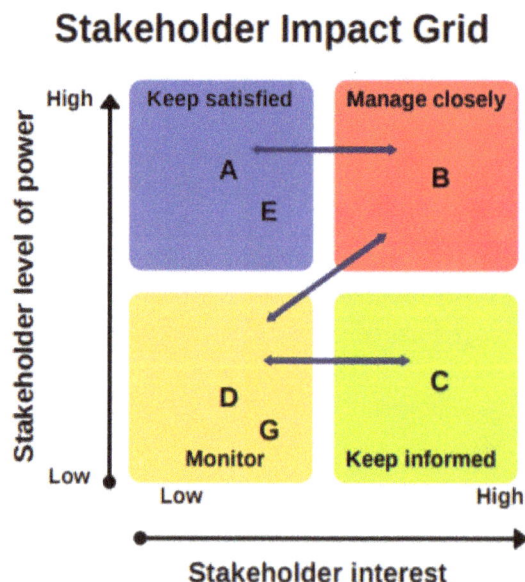

Figure 6.2 Stakeholder impact grid

Stakeholder analysis helps the project manager and the team to develop understanding and insight into the level of power and interest each stakeholder has on the project. Stakeholder analysis forms the backbone for strategising the engagement for maximum impact.

6.4 Engaging the stakeholders

You should by now understand how to identity and analyse stakeholders. This step is to develop a robust and effective method for communicating and engaging stakeholders.

Stakeholder engagement allows the project team to fully understand what the stakeholders want and/or need. It helps to find the most appropriate method for addressing their needs, reach a compromise or influence them, or reach a win-win situation.

Example: a powerful stakeholder may also have a high interest in the project; such stakeholders must be monitored very closely.

6.5 Communicating with stakeholders

Lack of stakeholder communication and engagement can cause stakeholders to slip from one **desirable position** into an **undesirable position** on the stakeholder impact grid.

Example: a very powerful and influential stakeholder with a high interest in a project can slip to having a low interest simply because of lack of engagement and communication. Engagement could be any of the following: meetings, presentations, demonstrations, discussions, etc.

To fully engage with all stakeholders appropriately, a **communication plan** should be developed.

Developing a **communication plan** is one way of documenting the strategy for effectively engaging stakeholders.

For example, during project delivery, stakeholders will require different levels of engagement. Some may need a face-to-face meeting, a formal meeting, others a simple email or phone update, or report, etc.

The emphasis is to make the communication and engagement relevant and appropriate to the stakeholder. Without proper engagement, stakeholders can sway from having a positive to a negative interest. For this reason, such stakeholders must be kept satisfied throughout the project.

Summary

Having read this chapter you should now be aware of and able to:

- Explain who stakeholders are
- State some of the techniques for identifying stakeholders
- Sketch a simple stakeholder grid to demonstrate power and interest
- Explain the meaning of a 'stakeholder management plan'
- Explain why communicating with stakeholders is important

End-of-chapter assessment – project stakeholders

Exercise 1 – Humanitarian mission project

Using the humanitarian mission project, can you reflect and list all the possible stakeholders for this project?

(Think about those who may be interested in the project, those who may not like to see the project happen or even those with information that can benefit the project.)

Exercise 2 – Humanitarian mission project

1   **Which of the following is not true about stakeholders?**
    A. Stakeholders are those who have an interest in the project
    B. Stakeholders are those who are impacted by the project
    C. Stakeholders can be internal or external to the organisation
    D. Stakeholders do not have the power to stop a project

2   **Stakeholders can either be in favour or oppose the project.**
    A. True
    B. False

3   **The project sponsor is also a stakeholder of the project.**
    A. True
    B. False

4   **The stakeholder engagement process follows this sequence:**
    A. Identification, Analysis, Engagement
    B. Planning, Identification, Engagement
    C. Analysis, Engagement, Communication
    D. Identification, Assessment, Communication

5   **The best approach to engage with stakeholders is to develop:**

       A. A communication plan

       B. Meeting minutes

       C. Consultation strategy

       D. Communication engagement plan

6   **A stakeholder impact grid is used to:**

       A. Group stakeholders in a grid

       B. Group stakeholders according to their interest in a project

       C. Group stakeholders according to their level of power in a project

       D. Group stakeholders according to their level of power and interest in a
          project

7   **Which of the following is not a reason for analysing stakeholders?**

       A. To understand the level of influence the stakeholder can have on the
          project

       B. To understand the level of power the stakeholders have in society

       C. To help the project manager to develop a suitable strategy to engage
          stakeholders

       D. All of the above

8   **You have recently joined a new project team as the project manager. The
       project you are working on has no record of stakeholder analysis. What
       will be the best thing to do?**

       A. Carry on as normal; the opportunity is lost

       B. Do not carry on; request to join another project team

       C. Identify all potential stakeholders and carry out an analysis as soon as
          possible

       D. A and B are correct

9   **Can a stakeholder who has no power but a lot of interest in your project
       influence another stakeholder with a lot of power to use this power to
       influence your project?**

       A. Yes

       B. No

CHAPTER 7

JUSTIFYING THE PROJECT INVESTMENT (BUSINESS CASE)

By the end of this chapter you should be able to:

– Explain what the business case is

– Explain the purpose of a business case

– Identify the content of a typical business case

– Explain who is involved in the creation of the business case

7.1 The business case

The business case is the document written to provide **justification** for undertaking a project.

To properly justify why a project should be undertaken, you must evaluate the **benefits, costs** and **risks** of **alternative options** and provide a basis or rationale for the **preferred solution/option**.

The business case is usually used to obtain senior management commitment and approval for investment in the project because it is an important document which fundamentally answers the question '**WHY**' a project is being undertaken.

The business case must be kept as a **live document** and updated when additional or updated project information becomes available. Because the business case is prepared early in the project, some of the information may be very high-level and not comprehensive; therefore, as the project progresses and new information becomes available, it must be captured and reflected in the business case.

The size, complexity, and scope of the project will usually determine how detailed the business case will be. For a small and simple project, the business case could be as simple as a few sentences to a page or couple of pages. Conversely, for large and complex projects, the business case can be several pages, a whole book or even a dossier.

7.2 Who owns the business case?

The business case is owned by the **project sponsor**. Although the project sponsor may delegate the writing of the business case to the project manager, another team or organisation, the sponsor ultimately approves and owns the business case and will be **accountable** for it.

Mostly the project manager will be responsible for preparing the business case on behalf of the project sponsor. Sometimes, depending on the project complexity, the project manager may also require specialist support in writing the business case; for example, the project manager may need input from technical experts, specialists, consultants, etc. to assist with addressing all the content of the business case.

Regardless of who provides information or writes the business case, the ultimate ownership, approval and accountability still rests with the project sponsor and they are responsible for ensuring that the benefits for which the project is being undertaken are documented and realised on completion of the project.

7.3 What the business case addresses

Before writing the business case, enough information must be gathered on the project to address the typical requirements for justifying the need for the project.

Table 7.1 The business case content

Risks	A high-level risk assessment of each option must be included.
Benefits/requirements	The expected high-level benefits should be known and recorded.
Scope	Include a high-level project scope.
Timescale	A high-level programme, with key milestones for each option, should be included.
Constraints	Most projects have constraints. It may well be that one option can be delivered only if we overcome strong opposition from a third party.
Financial appraisal	Each option will have an associated cost and the expected benefit possibly calculated in monetary terms, which is then used to work out the return on the investment. Various financial appraisals can be carried out.
Recommendation	A recommended option with justification to support it and why the business should invest in this option.

Table 7.2 What the business case addresses

The completed business case highlights the project objectives, the expected benefits, costs and justification for each project option considered	The risks of not doing the project or the risks associated with the option's discounted rate of return, etc.
High level project scope	It will usually conclude with a recommendation of the preferred option
Commercial evaluations (payback, return on investment, internal rate of return)	High level programme of works
Project constraints	The business case is owned by the project sponsor and is used to justify to senior leadership, investors, stakeholders, decision-makers, etc. why the project is viable and beneficial

7.4 The business case approval

In certain instances, the **project sponsor** may need to appear before a panel of decision-makers to explain the project and justify the benefits as well as elaborate on some of the assessment carried out to reach the recommendation.

Once the panel is satisfied with the justification, they will approve to progress the project to the next stage of the project cycle or make a recommendation.

Often the approval of the business case is associated with the release of funding to progress the project until the next gateway, or for the whole project.

Summary

Having read this chapter you should now be aware of and able to:

–   Explain what the business case is
–   Explain the purpose of a business case
–   Identify the content of a typical business case
–   Explain who is involved in the creation of the business case

End-of-chapter assessment – justifying the project

Exercise 1 – The humanitarian mission project

Using the humanitarian mission project, assume that you have carried out the necessary analysis, considered various options and have come to a point where you want to justify the preferred option. Prepare a brief justification for the preferred option.

Exercise 2 – The humanitarian mission project

1   **The document prepared and used to justify investment in the project is:**
     A. The business plan
     B. The business case
     C. The investment plan
     D. The justification plan

2   **Which of these is the output of the concept stage:**
     A. The project management plan
     B. The business plan
     C. The business case
     D. The justification plan

3   **Who is accountable for the business case?**
     A. The project manager
     B. The project sponsor
     C. The project team
     D. All of the above

4   **The project business case can be written by the project manager on behalf of the project sponsor.**
     A. True
     B. False

5   The business case is typically seen as the ……. for the project
         A. Justification
         B. Mandate
         C. Plan
         D. Strategy

6   The business case is used to address which of the following?
         A. Risks
         B. Timescale
         C. Scope
         D. All of the above

7   The business case is typically written during which project life cycle stage?
         A. Concept
         B. Development
         C. Deployment
         D. Handover and closeout

CHAPTER 8

THE PROJECT MANAGEMENT PLAN

By the end of this chapter you should be able to:

- State the main purpose of a project management plan
- Define who is involved in the creation of the project management plan
- List the typical content of a project management plan
- Outline the stakeholders of a project management plan
- Explain why the project management plan needs to be approved, owned and shared

8.1 The project management plan (PMP)

The PMP is sometimes referred to as the project initiation document (PID) or project execution plan (PEP), depending on which organisation you work for.

The project management plan is the document that brings together all the plans for a project. For example: how the project manager plans to manage risks, communication, quality, stakeholders, etc.

The purpose of preparing a PMP is to create a single document to record the outcomes of the planning process. The PMP can be used as the reference (baseline) for the project cost, time, quality, etc. The PMP is usually written and owned by the project manager.

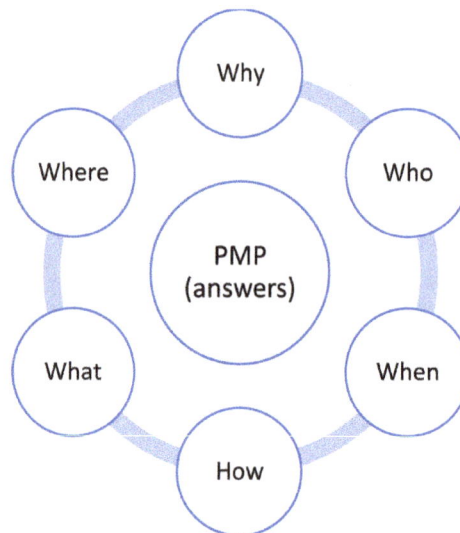

Figure 8.1 What the PMP addresses

This will include:

- Agreed project scope/deliverables
- Organisational structure
- Agreed project cost
- Agreed project timescale/schedule
- How risks will be managed
- How changes will be managed
- What quality it will be delivered to
- How resources will be procured
- How communication will be managed
- How stakeholders will be managed
- Project assumptions and constraints

Table 8.1 What the PMP addresses

Why	Description of project, requirements, objectives
What	Project scope, specification, acceptance criteria, KPIs, etc.
When	Schedule/programme, key milestones
How	Delivery method, HSE plans, communication plans, risk management
Who	Roles, authority, delegation, organogram, etc.
Where	Where the project is taking place

8.2 What to include in the project management plan (PMP)

The content of the PMP is usually not fixed. It may vary within different organisations to suit their processes. However, as a minimum, the PMP should address the following:

o RISK MANAGEMENT
o SCHEDULE
o QUALITY MANAGEMENT
o COST MANAGEMENT

The PMP can also address other important areas that will be fundamental to the project delivery, including stakeholder engagement, change management, issue management, etc.

The PMP must be kept as a **live document,** kept up to date and version-controlled when new and updated information becomes available.

8.3 The PMP stakeholders

The PMP is prepared and owned by the project manager but **approved by the sponsor.**

Although the project manager owns and is accountable for the project management plan, it should be developed with the wider project team members.

Some specialist planning expertise may be provided by a support function; for example, specialists, technical experts, subject matter experts, supply chain, contractors, estimators, users, etc.

As the project manager, it is useful to engage and involve other stakeholders when writing the PMP. Engaging stakeholders ensures commitment and ownership of the plan.

The completed PMP should be agreed and signed off by the project sponsor. Once agreed, the PMP serves as a **baseline** for delivering the project and for reporting against.

The PMP is used to serve as a common understanding and agreement between the **project manager, stakeholders and sponsor.**

On completion, the PMP should be shared with relevant stakeholders. This ensures **each stakeholder is fully aware and understands what the project will deliver and how they will be delivered.**

8.4 The PMP as the deployment project baseline

> **Baseline** is 'the reference levels against which a project, programme or portfolio is monitored and controlled' - (Murray-Webster, Dalcher and Association for Project Management, 2019).

✓ The **baseline** in simple terms refers to the fixed starting (reference) point from where the cost, schedule and scope etc. for the project can be measured.

✓ The PMP, once prepared, serves as the baseline for the project.

✓ Projects can be affected by different factors, like cost, time, etc. This means that any change with any of these can be measured against the reference point. The baseline will therefore provide a good reference point to measure these changes against.

✓ For example, a project set out to complete by a specific date (set as the baseline completion) could be judged as completed early or late if the actual completion date is measured or compared to the agreed baseline date.

See the table below for a demonstration of baseline using a school coursework.

Table 8.2 Project baseline illustration

	Scenario one	Scenario two
Agreed submission date (baseline date)	30th May	30th May
Actual date submitted	27th May	7th June
Difference	3 days early	8 days late

The **deployment baseline** goes beyond baselining cost and time to include quality, estimates, scope, and risk baselines.

8.5 Deployment baselines and project life cycles

As discussed earlier, projects can be delivered using several types of life cycle approaches, including **linear, iterative, hybrid** or **extended life cycle.**

A **linear project life cycle** is usually adopted when enough detail is known about the project and the scope is well understood. Adopting a linear project life cycle also means the project **baselines** can be set from the outset, allowing little room to change as the project progresses.

Changes in time, scope and quality can be measured and monitored as the project progresses through the linear life cycle.

Conversely, with an **iterative life cycle,** the scope and quality expectations cannot be fixed from the beginning of the project. This makes it difficult to have a reference point for baselining. An iterative life cycle tends to use the amount of resources and time as the baseline. Time is used by applying timeboxing as a measure of deviation from the baseline.

Once baselines are set for resources, time, quality, scope, etc., they are recorded in the PMP to serve as the reference point for delivering the project.

Table 8.3 Scope comparison between linear and iterative life cycle

Linear life cycle	Iterative life cycle
Project scope is firmed up/well defined at the early stages of the project	Scope unclear and develops as the project goes through several iterations
Baseline scope is set early on in the project	Baseline scope cannot be set because it is unclear
Baseline time can be set	Baseline time can be set. Timeboxing is used
Baseline requirements are set from the start	Baseline requirements develop as the project goes through several iterations
Baseline resources are set	Baseline resources are set
Quality expectations are set as baseline	Quality cannot be set as baseline until several iterations have happened
Driven by scope and quality	Driven by resource usage

Summary

Having read this chapter you should now be aware of and able to:

- State the main purpose of a project management plan
- Define who is involved in the creation of the project management plan
- List the typical content of a project management plan

- Outline the stakeholders of a project management plan
- Explain why the project management plan needs to be approved, owned and shared

End-of-chapter assessment – project management plan

Exercise 1 – The humanitarian mission project

Using the humanitarian mission project, write a brief **project management plan**. Your plan should outline how you are going to manage this project, including how you will manage risk, costs, schedule, quality and stakeholders.

(Consider some of the headings already discussed in this chapter.)

Exercise 2 – The humanitarian mission project

1   **The purpose of the project management plan is to?**
     A. Plan the project deliverables
     B. Ensure the project manager has a good plan for managing the project
     C. Document the outcome of the project planning process
     D. Give the project manager confidence when managing the project

2   **The project management plan (PMP) is sometimes referred to as the:**
     A. Project establishment plan (PEP)
     B. Project development plan (PDP)
     C. Project executive plan (PEP)
     D. Project execution plan (PEP)

3   **The PMP is prepared and owned by:**
     A. The project organisation
     B. The project manager
     C. The department managing the project
     D. The person who writes the plan

4   **Which of the following will the PMP not address?**

A. Risk

B. Schedule

C. Cost

D. Project life cycle

5   **The PMP once written should be approved by the sponsor because:**

A. The sponsor is the project manager's line manager

B. The sponsor may need to check the grammar

C. The sponsor is ultimately responsible for the benefits the project will deliver and must be happy with how it is delivered

D. The sponsor must pay the project manager for writing it

6   **The project deployment baseline can best be explained as:**

A. The start date for monitoring the project

B. The project reference point

C. The reference levels for monitoring the project

D. The reference levels for monitoring the project cost and time

7   **Which of the following can be a stakeholder of the PMP?**

A. The project sponsor

B. The project team

C. Suppliers

D. All of the above

CHAPTER 9

QUALITY (FITNESS FOR PURPOSE)

By the end of this chapter you should be able to:

- Define the term 'quality'
- Outline the purpose of quality management
- Define the term 'quality planning'
- Define the term 'quality control'
- Outline the purpose of quality assurance

9.1 Quality management

> **Quality management** 'A discipline for ensuring the outputs, benefits and the processes by which they are delivered, meet stakeholder requirements and are fit for purpose' - (Association for Project Management, 2012).

Have you ever had a product or service delivered to you that you judged to be of poor or inferior quality? Perhaps your expectation and interpretation of quality was different from whoever provided the service or product.

This scenario supports the fact that we all have our own individual quality expectations and interpretations. This may be influenced by certain factors, like our knowledge, experience and exposure, etc.

What may be interpreted as quality to one person may not be to another, therefore determining and agreeing project quality is crucial if you want to avoid user disappointment and stakeholders refusing to accept the finished project.

Quality should be planned, managed and controlled such that the project ends up with products and services which are fit for purpose and in line with the stakeholders'/ clients' expectations and requirements.

> '**Quality** is the fitness for purpose or the degree of conformance of the outputs of a process or the process itself to the requirements' - (Murray-Webster, Dalcher and Association for Project Management, 2019).

9.1.1 Quality can be expensive

Quality does not just happen unless specific steps, processes and methods are followed that will lead to the expected project output. To achieve a certain quality may require following meticulous processes and using, and/or adhering to, specific standards, processes, requirements, steps, etc.

All these may take extra time, cost more money and/or require more resource over and above the norm. For example, developing a given product to a recognised international, European, British or American standard, etc. may place specific demands and requirements to be followed. Doing so does not only ensure compliance to the standard but also ensures a certain expected level of quality.

It also implies that the additional stringent processes, steps, etc. will translate into more cost over and above a similar product which is not being delivered to the same standard.

Two projects may deliver the same outputs with different levels of quality if the specified processes and methods are altered.

To arrive at the expected quality will require **planning, monitoring, testing** and **continuous improvement**. All these steps can make quality delivery very expensive.

Having a poor quality product may not be necessarily cheaper if you consider the direct and indirect cost of regular repair, maintenance and rework. Sometimes poor quality goods and services can lead to reputational damage, accidents, prosecutions, expensive repairs, recalls, etc.

Quality management steps involve:

Step 1 – Planning how quality will be achieved (**quality planning**)
Step 2 – Making sure the planned quality is achieved (**quality assurance**)
Step 3 – Testing the product or service to make sure it meets the expected quality (**quality control**)
Step 4 – Learning your lessons and improving your quality processes (**continuous improvement**)

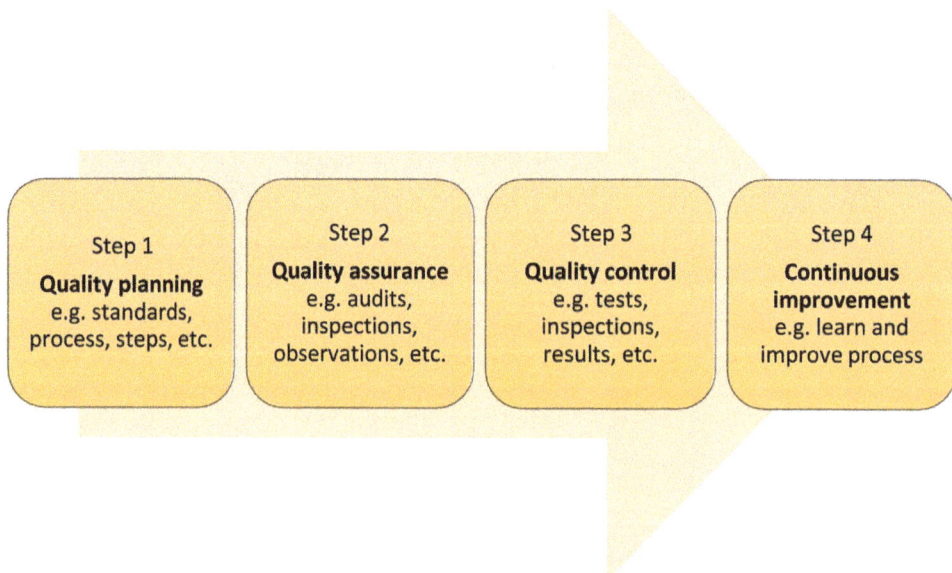

Step 1	Step 2	Step 3	Step 4
Quality planning e.g. standards, process, steps, etc.	**Quality assurance** e.g. audits, inspections, observations, etc.	**Quality control** e.g. tests, inspections, results, etc.	**Continuous improvement** e.g. learn and improve process

Figure 9.1 Quality management process

9.2 Quality planning

> '**Quality planning** takes the defined scope and specifies the acceptance criteria used to validate that the outputs are fit for purpose to the sponsor' - (Murray-Webster, Dalcher and Association for Project Management, 2019).

Quality planning is the process of ensuring that the project **outputs** and the **processes** used to achieve them will result in the quality the stakeholders expect and require, or that the product and service will be fit for the purpose for which it is intended.

Quality will not naturally happen unless it is carefully planned.

Quality planning will include specifying the **standards, steps, actions, processes** and **resources,** etc. that will together deliver or ensure the expected quality.

In project management, the various standards and specifications to which the project deliverables/outputs should be delivered can all be documented in the QUALITY PLAN. The plan determines the level of quality expected and the steps or processes to be followed to guarantee that quality. For example, following an internationally recognised standard like the American standard, British standard, European standard, etc. ensures consistent quality is achieved at all times because such standards are proven, tried and tested over time.

In chapter one of this book the project triangle was explained, which showed **quality** as one of the attributes of the project constraints. The others are cost, time and risk.

When planning to deliver quality, the simplest quality requirement or statement could be along the lines of being '**fit for purpose**'. This may be a broad statement but will at least cover many unforeseen issues with the output.

Quality goes beyond making statements of compliance to specific standards, steps, processes, actions, etc. and hope that they will be attained.

A series of additional processes and steps must be followed to ensure that each stage of the delivery process conforms and aligns with the specific quality expectation.

For example, the quality of a concrete foundation will depend on the proportion of cement, sand, aggregate and water, including the curing period allowed. Following this process and using approved proportions will ensure a certain quality of concrete. Likewise, any deviation from the standard will impact on the expected quality and may result in defects.

9.3 Quality assurance

> **Quality assurance** consists of inspections, measurements, testing, and procedures followed during the delivery process to ensure that the project outputs meet acceptance criteria defined during quality planning.

The next step in the quality process which follows the planning stage is the monitoring. The process, steps and activities for delivering the product and service must be carefully monitored. This is the QUALITY ASSURANCE stage.

It is best to agree upfront what must be checked, provided, seen, tested, etc. during the delivery of the product/service to ensure quality.

Quality assurance generally is a demonstration that the quality process is being followed as planned.

Examples of quality assurance activities include:

- ☐ Periodic inspections
- ☐ Audits
- ☐ Asking questions
- ☐ Observations

9.4 Quality control

> '**Quality control** consists of inspection, measurement and testing to verify that the project outputs meet acceptance criteria defined during quality planning' - (Murray-Webster, Dalcher and Association for Project Management, 2019)

QUALITY CONTROL is the third step in the project quality management process. This comes into effect only when the project is complete. The deliverables will be tested to determine if the quality expectations in the plans have been met.

Sometimes you may not necessarily have to test the product or output yourself if you are not qualified to do so.

As a client or stakeholder, you could ask to see things like test certificates as confirmation of quality, or you can engage the services of an independent qualified person or body to certify conformance.

Other criteria can also be used to test if quality expectations have been met. For example:

☐ Visual inspection
☐ Independent tests
☐ Test certificates/results
☐ Design calculations
☐ Laboratory results, etc.

9.5 The difference between quality assurance and quality control

Table 9.1 Difference between quality assurance and quality control

QUALITY ASSURANCE	QUALITY CONTROL
A **proactive** approach focused on the process and ensures mistakes/defects are prevented	A **reactive** approach focused on the end product and ensures any mistakes/defects are identified
Used to improve the process for achieving the deliverables	Used to find and eliminate sources of defects within the process
Is the responsibility of every person/team member involved in the process	A small dedicated team may be responsible for testing the quality.
Used to prevent problems with quality **during** delivery/manufacture, etc.	Used as a tool for correcting mistakes **after** delivery/manufacture, etc.
Ensures a good quality system is in place for product delivery.	Helps to provide feedback on the process and the causes behind quality problems.

Summary

Having read this chapter you should now be aware of and able to:

– Define the term 'quality'
– Outline the purpose of quality management
– Define the term 'quality planning'

– Define the term 'quality control'
– Outline the purpose of quality assurance

End-of-chapter assessment – quality management

Exercise 1 – The humanitarian mission project

Using the case study topic of the humanitarian mission project, reflect on how you could deliver a mission that is fit for purpose. As the project manager, you want to draft your quality requirement for inclusion in the PMP. What will be your expectations and how will you go about testing and confirming that they are met?

Exercise 2 – The humanitarian mission project

1   The purpose of project quality management is to:

    A. Have long-lasting products

    B. Ensure project deliverables are fit for purpose

    C. Ensure the project adheres to relevant standards

    D. Provide confidence that the project manager knows what they are doing

2   The project quality management process follows this sequence:

    A. Quality planning, quality control, quality assurance, continuous improvement

    B. Quality control, quality assurance, quality planning, continuous improvement

    C. Quality assurance, quality planning, quality control, continuous improvement

    D. Quality planning, quality assurance, quality control, continuous improvement

3   **Which of the following is not a quality assurance activity?**

A. Inspection

B. Observation

C. Interviews

D. Independent testing

4   **Quality generally means:**

A. Fit for sale

B. Fit for purpose

C. Long-lasting

D. Attractive and robust

5   **Managing quality generally means ensuring the project outputs and benefits, and the process used to achieve them, meet the stakeholder requirements and are fit for purpose.**

A. True

B. False

6   **The difference between quality control and quality assurance is:**

A. Quality control happens after the project and assurance is during the project

B. Quality control happens during the project and assurance after the project

C. Quality assurance and control are carried out by the project manager

D. A and C are correct

7   **Quality assurance is not:**

A. A proactive approach focused on the process

B. Used to improve the process for achieving deliverables

C. Used to prevent problems with quality during delivery

D. A reactive approach focused on the end product

CHAPTER 10

THE PROJECT REQUIREMENTS

By the end of this chapter you should be able to:

– Define the term 'requirement'

– Define the term 'requirement management'

– Outline the steps involved in writing a good project requirement

– Explain why the project manager needs to develop SMART requirements

10.1 Requirements

> **Requirements** are all the things that are wanted or needed by the stakeholders, customers, users, clients, etc. These can be defined and categorised using the must-haves, should-haves, could-haves, and won't-haves of the project.

Have you ever found yourself in a situation where your requirements/needs for a job were misinterpreted or misunderstood, leading to a product or service that did not meet your expectations? You may be very much aware that a lot of project misunderstanding and confusion originate from unclear or misunderstood project requirements.

When project requirements (needs and wants) are not fully understood and agreed, this can lead to a situation where the stakeholders can refuse to accept the project deliverables. The implications are wasted time and effort, disappointment and expensive rework, along with protracted dialogue even after the project has been completed and, in some cases, formal dispute and arbitration.

As the project professional, you must remember that you are not delivering project requirements based on what you want or think should be delivered but on what the stakeholders need or want and have agreed with you.

10.2 Requirement management

> **Requirement management** is the process of capturing, assessing, and justifying what the customers, users, clients, stakeholders want, or need. They are caught using the must-haves, should-haves, could-haves, and won't-haves of the project

Requirement management is an essential project management technique.

For example, if your requirement for a car is one with red leather seating, you may not accept pink leather seating as an alternative, depending on how important the red leather seating is to you.

Customer: I need a car for
commuting to work

Supplier: I have
something in mind

Figure 10.1 Project requirement illustration

This example goes to demonstrate that when describing project requirements, it is useful to be clear and, where possible, ensure each requirement is assessed and prioritised into:

- ✓ Must have
- ✓ Should have
- ✓ Could have
- ✓ Won't have

Categorising your requirements as above helps to focus the project delivery and decide on trade-offs.

In addition to the prioritisation above, you should be mindful of the impact each of the priorities can also have on project **time, cost, quality, risk,** etc.

For example, making a requirement for a triple-glazed window on a house-building project a 'must have' could impact on the overall project cost compared to making it a 'could have' requirement.

10.3 Characteristics of good project requirements

- ✓ Clear and unambiguous
- ✓ Should be specific

✓ Should be measurable
✓ Should be realistic
✓ Should be possible to be achieved within the expected timeframe
✓ Are usually linked to the project benefits
✓ Are usually linked to the project scope
✓ Should be analysed, assessed and justified for inclusion
✓ Can be stated in the form of benefits, performance, statements, etc.

Summary

Having read this chapter you should now be aware of and able to:

–   Define the term 'requirement'
–   Define requirement management
–   Outline the steps involved in writing a good project requirement
–   Explain why the project manager needs to develop SMART requirements

End-of-chapter assessment – project requirements

Exercise 1 – The humanitarian mission project

a. Using the humanitarian mission project, write down some of the project requirements you will expect as a client. Make use of the must haves, should haves and could haves etc.

b. Use the list you have prepared to create a simple work breakdown structure (WBS) for the humanitarian mission.

Exercise 2 – The humanitarian mission project

1   The project requirement can best be explained as:

    A. Stakeholders' wants and needs

    B. Stakeholders' desires

    C. Clients' wants and needs

    D. Clients' desires and wishes

2   One technique a project manager will use to define project requirements is by categorising them; which of these is not relevant?

    A. Must have

    B. Should have

    C. We have

    D. Can't have

3   The project requirements should be:

    A. SMART

    B. Directly linked to project benefits

    C. Analysed and justified

    D. All of the above

4   **The process of capturing, assessing and justifying stakeholders' wants and needs is referred to as:**

A. Requirement planning

B. Requirement assessment

C. Requirement management

D. None of the above

CHAPTER 11

UNDERSTANDING THE PROJECT SCOPE

By the end of this chapter you should be able to:

- Define the term 'scope management'

- Differentiate between scope management within linear projects and scope

- Describe how product breakdown structures (PBS) and work breakdown structures (WBS) are used to illustrate the required scope of work

- Outline how a project manager would use cost breakdown structures (CBS), organisational breakdown structures (OBS) and the responsibility assignment matrix (RAM)

11.1 Scope

> **Scope** is all the project deliverables and the amount of work involved in achieving them.

Scope is one of the most common terminologies you will come across in project management. Most people confuse **scope** with **requirements**, but the two are different. The **scope** of a project identifies what should be delivered (**deliverables**) and the associated work (**things to do**) to achieve it.

To write a proper scope statement, you also need to understand the project **requirements** and **benefits** because they both help in identifying, defining and controlling the project scope. The project **requirements** describe the functionalities and the capabilities of what should be delivered; simply put, they are the **wants** and **needs** of the stakeholders.

For example, if a project deliverable is to install windows in a house, some of the requirements could be: window type (double-glazed or triple-glazed, timber-framed, PVC, etc.), colour, size, manufacturer and finish. The list goes on.

If you can recollect what was explained about the project triangle in chapter one, you will notice that the scope of a project is at the **centre** of the project constraints. This means that the scope of a project can affect the cost, time and quality of the project.

As the project is delivered, it is important to keep a very close eye on scope changes through a proper **change control** process (see chapter 16). This ensures changes are assessed for their impact on the project scope.

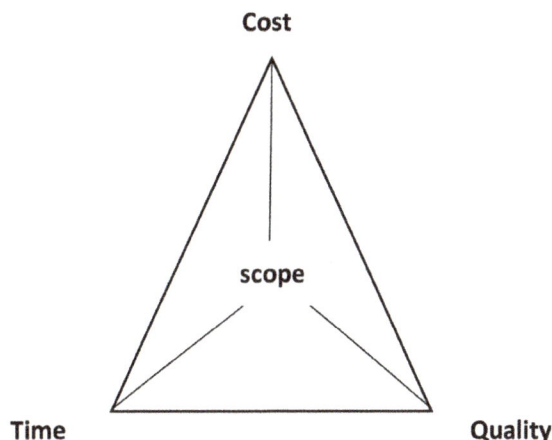

Figure 11.1 The project triangle

Another example of a scope statement: **design and build a three-bedroom house with two bathrooms and a garage.** This scope statement will generate specific project requirements which may include specific functionalities or capabilities the building should have or be able to do, including the type of finish, flooring type, door type, specific types of ironmongery, etc.

The project scope statement summarises what is to be delivered by the project.

It can be concluded that the **scope** of a project is not only what should be delivered as the end product, but also encompasses the work required.

This means a change in a project scope can affect the project's **final cost, quality, success criteria** and **timescale.**

In the house-building example, the work involved, resources and cost of building the house will be directly linked to the project **scope.** Any change in the requirements from, say, a three-bedroom to a four-bedroom with a garage and basement, will imply more work, more resource and more time required to complete the building, which will therefore mean a change in scope.

To write and understand the project **scope,** you must also understand that the scope is not a standalone item of project deliverables. It is usually linked and interrelated with other aspects of the project, like:

– **Requirements**: stakeholders' wants and needs
– **Solutions to the requirements**: solutions for achieving the requirements
– **Benefits**: stakeholders' wants and needs expressed as benefits
– **Transformation of business-as-usual activities** to make use of the project to realise the benefits
– **Configuration management**: changes to configuration items affect scope

All of these have a role to play in determining or affecting the project scope.

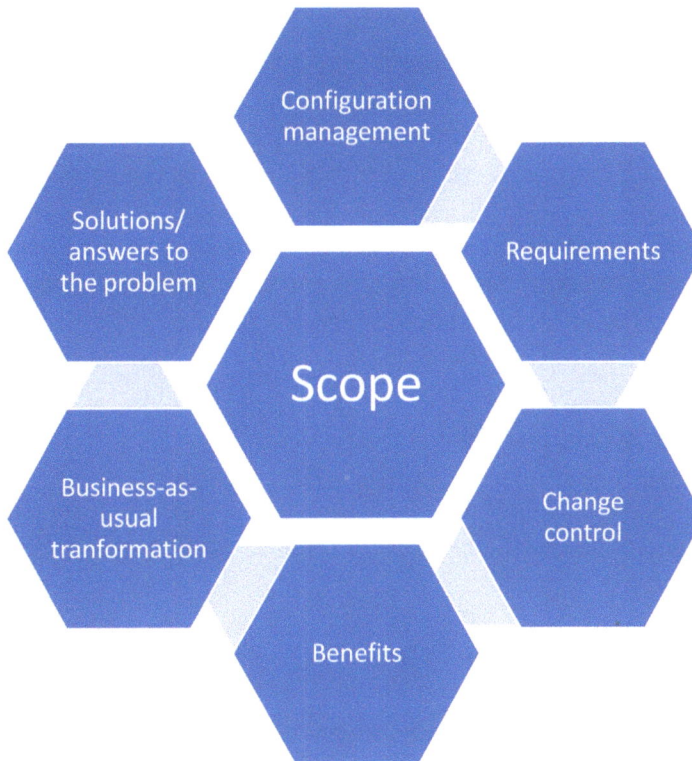

Figure 11.2 The project scope linkages

11.2 Project life cycles' impact on scope

The project life cycle has an impact on the project scope. As we have learnt from the life cycles (chapter four), a **linear life cycle** is usually used when the scope (the project outputs and the work involved) is known and well defined.

Conversely, an iterative life cycle is used when the scope is not clear and well defined. For this reason, the scope of an iterative project cannot be fixed from the start but can be set as a target scope or broken down into the must haves, should haves, could haves and can't haves.

11.3 Scope creep

Whenever a change to any aspect of the project is required, a proper assessment of the impact of this change on the project cost, time and quality should be carried out. Where applicable, relevant adjustments to the cost, time and quality will be made.

Sometimes the project manager may be expected to accommodate changes on a project using the previously agreed budget, time and quality expectations.

This means the changes are to be incorporated into the project without any corresponding adjustment to **cost, time** and **quality** to reflect the impact of that change. This is **SCOPE CREEP** because there is a gradual change to the project scope from what was agreed.

Sometimes, irrespective of the scope change, the budget may be expected to remain unchanged as per the baseline. Should this be the case, a compromise according to the project cost, time and quality should be reached.

> **Scope management** is the process for finding, clarifying, and controlling the project deliverables.

11.4 Work breakdown structure (WBS)

It is easier to think that the scope of a project can only be the written statements of what is to be delivered or not delivered. Though correct, you should also note that the scope of any project can be broken down into things to do, or smaller sub-products, using a hierarchical structure like: **WBS** and **PBS.**

The **work breakdown structure** and the **product breakdown structure** both give a clearer roadmap of the smaller tasks/products that combine in a sequential and hierarchical order to deliver the ultimate product or deliverable.

The WBS is usually shown in a hierarchical structure using different levels. The top level represents the end product, e.g. house, car, wedding, party, etc.

The second level represents the **tangible deliverables,** which are subsets of the top level.

The third and any subsequent levels represent the work required (things to do) to produce the deliverables listed in level two.

In other words, the work breakdown structure is the hierarchy of all the work to be completed from the lowest activity through to when the final product or output will be delivered.

Main project deliverable — Level 1

Sub deliverable 1 | Sub deliverable 2 | Sub deliverable 3 — Level 2

Task 1.1 | Task 1.2 | Task 2.1 | Task 2.2 | Task 3.1 | Task 3.2 — Level 3

Sub task 3.2.1 | Sub task 3.2.2 — Level 4

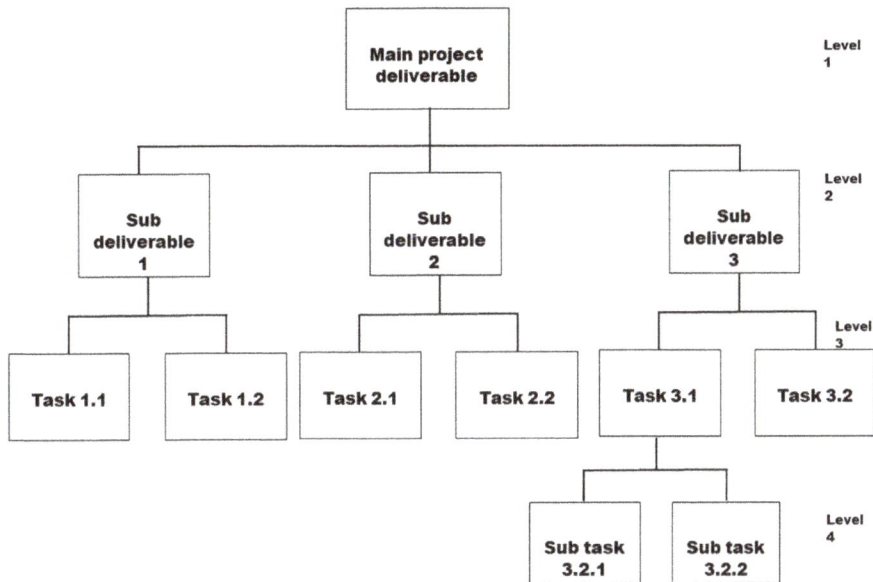

Figure 11.3 The work breakdown structure illustration

11.4.1 Why the work breakdown structure?

✓ The work breakdown structure (WBS) is similar to the product breakdown structure (PBS). Both provide a solid foundation for planning and arranging the order of the work activities of the project (scheduling).
✓ The WBS breaks down the project into manageable work packages (to-do items) or activities.
✓ It provides an easier approach for estimating project costs accurately.
✓ It ensures important deliverables are not missed.
✓ It helps project managers to allocate project resources effectively.

11.5 Product breakdown structure (PBS)

✓ The product breakdown structure (PBS) is another method for representing the project scope. It is a hierarchical breakdown of the products, starting with the main product at the top and subdividing at each sub-level to show the components that make up the level above.
✓ The PBS can be broken down until you get to the very lowest level that shows the individual products. In other words, the PBS decomposes the products into smaller parts.

11.6 Cost breakdown structure (CBS)

✓ The cost breakdown structure (CBS) is similar to the work breakdown structure in terms of the hierarchical structure.
✓ The CBS allocates the cost to the individual work packages (things to do) identified in the WBS. The costs could be material costs, labour costs, hiring costs, other fees, equipment costs, etc.
✓ For larger and complex projects, the individual work packages can be assigned to a COST CODE/COST CENTRE for allocating all costs associated with that work package.

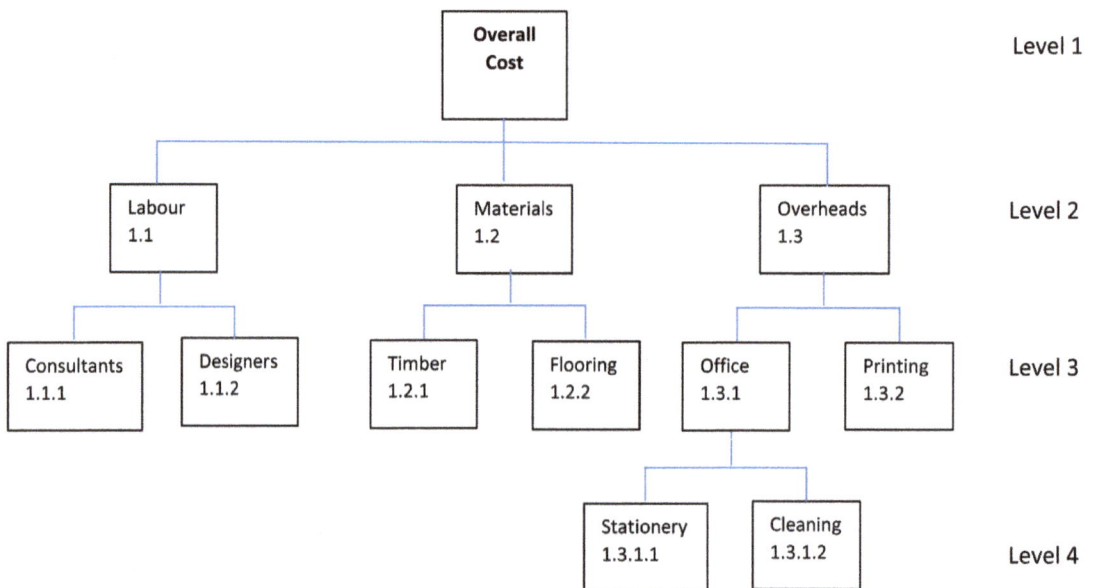

Figure 11.4 The project cost breakdown illustration

11.7 Organisational breakdown structure (OBS)

The organisational breakdown structure (OBS) is used in scope management to show a breakdown of the management groups, the reporting relationships and the communication channels during project delivery.

The chart below shows a very simple organisational breakdown structure for project delivery:

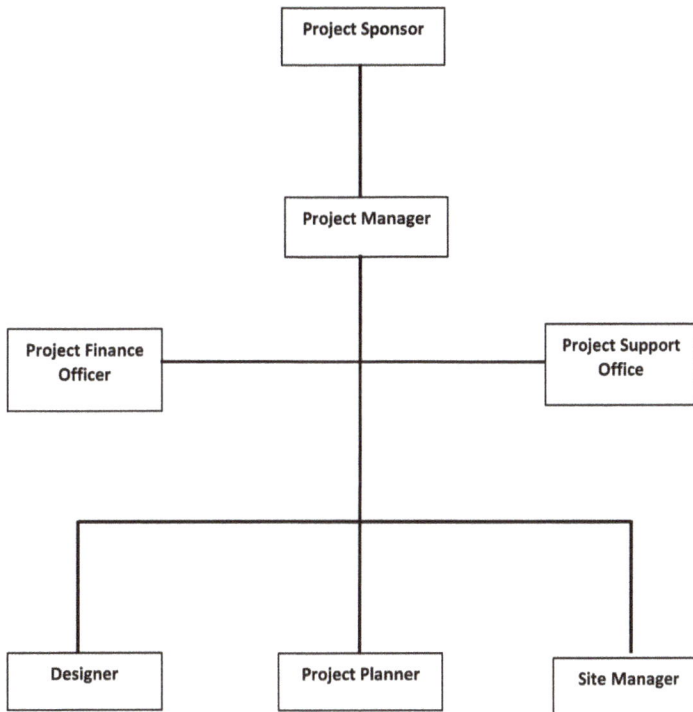

Figure 11.5 A simple project organogram

11.8 Responsibility assignment matrix

✓ The **project organisational breakdown structure** can be extended and combined with the **work breakdown structure** to create a detailed structure showing who is responsible for which work package (to-do item) in a project.

✓ This resulting structure is known as the RESPONSIBILITY ASSIGNMENT MATRIX (RAM). Individuals and teams can be allocated to tasks and deliverables using the RAM.

✓ Tasks are allocated according to who is accountable, responsible, consulted or informed.

RESPONSIBLE (R)	The person(s) who does the work
ACCOUNTABLE (A)	The person or team answerable for this work. They are the final approvers of the work
CONSULT (C)	Those whose opinions and views are sought
INFORM (I)	Those we must keep updated on progress or completion

	Project Manager	Site Manager	Labourer	Painter
Design	Accountable	Responsible	Inform	Inform
Delivery	Accountable	Inform	Responsible	Inform
Surface preparation	Consult	Accountable	Responsible	Inform
Painting	Accountable	Consult	Inform	Responsible
Inventory	Accountable	Responsible	Accountable	Inform
Cleaning	Inform	Inform	Responsible	Accountable

Figure 11.6 Project RACI illustration

Summary

Having read this chapter you should now be aware of and able to:

– Define the term 'scope management'
– Differentiate between scope management within linear projects and scope
– Describe how product breakdown structures and work breakdown structures are used to illustrate the required scope of work
– Outline how a project manager would use cost breakdown structures, organisational breakdown structures and the responsibility assignment matrix

End-of-chapter assessment – project scope

Exercise 1 – The humanitarian mission project

a. Using the humanitarian mission project, assume the main deliverable is temporary accommodation, subdivide this main deliverable into sub-deliverables. Further break the sub-deliverables into work activities that should be completed to achieve the sub-deliverables.

b. Use the list you have prepared to create a simple work breakdown structure for the humanitarian mission.

Exercise 2 – The humanitarian mission project

1   **The project scope can be explained as:**

A. The process whereby outputs, outcomes and benefits are identified, defined and controlled

B. The stakeholders' wants and needs

C. All the things to be delivered as part of the project, including the work required

D. All of the above

2   **Which of the following cannot be used to define the project scope:**

A. Work breakdown structure (WBS)

B. Product breakdown structure (PBS)

C. Organisational breakdown structure (OBS)

D. Responsibility assignment matrix (RAM)

3   **The cost breakdown structure:**

A. Allocates costs to the individual work packages

B. Allocates costs to the deliverables

C. Allocates costs to the resources

D. All of the above

4   An organisational breakdown structure (OBS) is used in scope management to:

A. Show the project manager's rank in project delivery

B. Show a breakdown of management groups

C. Show the reporting relationships and communication channels

D. Only B and C are correct

5   The responsibility assignment matrix (RAM) is created from a combination of:

A. WBS and CBS

B. PBS and WBS

C. OBS and WBS

D. None of the above

6   The term RACI in the responsibility assignment matrix (RAM) means:

A. Responsible, Accountable, Consult, Inform

B. Required, Action owner, Consult, Implement

C. Raise, Adapt, Confirm, Inspect

D. Responsible, Accountable, Confirm, Inform

7   When the scope of a project is well defined, which life cycle approach will you recommend?

A. Iterative life cycle

B. Linear life cycle

C. Iterative and linear life cycle

D. All of the above

8   Scope creep usually happens when:

A. The scope can no longer be defined

B. The scope gradually changes from what has been agreed

C. The scope exponentially changes during implementation

D. B and C are correct

9   The scope of a project is linked to all of the following, except:

A. Time

B. Cost

C. Resource

D. Quality

10   Which of the following will not play a role in determining the project scope?

A. Expected project benefits

B. Project requirements

C. Project changes

D. The project manager's experience

CHAPTER 12

SCHEDULING THE PROJECT ACTIVITIES

By the end of this chapter you should be able to:

- State the purpose of scheduling
- State the purpose of critical path analysis
- State the purpose of milestones
- Define the term 'timeboxing'

12.1 Scheduling

> **Schedule** is the timetable for showing the planned start and finish dates for project activities or events.

The building blocks of any project are the sum of all the individual work packages (to-do list) that must be carried out in an orderly way, either sequentially or concurrently, to deliver the project output. In project management, the **technique** for arranging these building blocks (**to-do list**) in such a way that allows optimum project performance is called **SCHEDULING.**

Scheduling deals with the methodical, sequential and/or concurrent arrangement of the individual project activities (to-do list) from start to finish. In other words, a schedule can also be simply termed as the **timetable** for a project because it shows when project activities and milestones are planned to start and complete over a period of time.

Scheduling in project management also requires an understanding of and the use of milestones and baselines (see chapter eight). A schedule can be shown using: **a Gantt chart, bar chart** or **a tabular listing of dates and activities.**

There are more advanced tools and software for scheduling; however, these are beyond the scope of this book and therefore will not be discussed.

12.2 Making use of activities' logical relationships

Scheduling goes beyond having a start and an end date for the work packages (things to do). To schedule a project first requires an understanding of all the activities (things to do) that make up the full project. This means a good understanding of and the use of the work breakdown structure (WBS) (see chapter 11) to assist with developing a good project schedule.

The WBS can simply be explained as all the work required to complete the project. A proper project schedule will use the work activities (work breakdown structure) to create a **logical sequence** and relationship between the activities. This is called the **LOGICAL RELATIONSHIP.**

For example, carpeting a newly built house cannot start until all the painting is completed in the rooms. This sequence of painting the rooms before carpeting may be the best **logical sequence,** instead of carpeting before painting.

This painting/carpeting sequence could further be refined to bring some efficiency. This can be done by establishing how soon the carpeting can start after the painting has started. Perhaps a few days after the painting starts the carpeting can also start, instead of waiting for the full house to be painted.

It can be concluded that the best **logical relationship** between carpeting and painting can further be explored to give the project the best chance of completing efficiently.

The following options can be explored:

o   The earliest date the painting can be finished to allow the carpeting to start
o   The earliest or latest date the painting can start or be extended without affecting the start of the carpet installation, etc.

Project activities generally follow four basic logical sequences:

Table 12.1 The project logical sequence clarification

Activity	Description	Example
Finish to Start (**FS**)	Where activity A must finish before activity B can start	You must finish dressing before you can start driving the car
Start to Start (**SS**)	Where activity B can only start when activity A has started	You can only start the publicity campaign after the project has started on site
Finish to Finish (**FF**)	Where activity B can only finish when activity A has finished	Publicity can only finish after the project has finished
Start to Finish (**SF**)	Where activity A must start before activity B can finish (rarely used)	Start the publicity before the project finishes.

The table above can also be explained diagrammatically as:

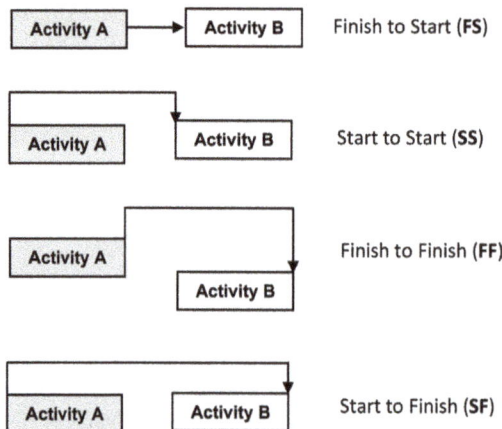

Figure 12.1 Project logical sequences

The above relationships allow a sequence that truly reflects the logical possibilities of delivering the project. Once all activity relationships have been logically determined, the next key step will be to determine the resources required to deliver these tasks/activities.

Scheduling can be used to deploy resources efficiently across the project. Using the work breakdown structure will assist with determining the resource required for each activity.

> *Scheduling is used to determine the overall project duration and when activities and events are planned to happen*

12.3 Understanding network diagrams

✓ You should by now have a good understanding of project scheduling and why project activities should be logically linked to each other.
✓ In simple terms, the network diagram is a graphical illustration of the logical sequence of all the project activities from start to finish.
✓ When constructing a network diagram, each project activity (to-do item) will be represented diagrammatically, as below. This will form the basis for creating a logically linked network diagram.
✓ Each activity can be represented by a diagram like this one

Earliest Start (ES)	Duration	Earliest Finish (EF)
Task ID		
Latest Start (LS)	Total Float (TF)	Latest Finish (LF)

1st April Earliest start	Duration 15 days	16th April Earliest finish
Installing a new garden shed		
15th May Latest start	45 days Total float	30th May Latest finish

5:30am Earliest start	Duration 4 hrs	9:30am Earliest arrival
Journey to an event starting at 10am		
6:00am Latest start	30 min Total float	10:00am Latest arrival

Figure 12.2 Network diagram illustration

Example calculation

Table 12.2 Project logical sequence demonstration

Earliest Finish	=	Earliest Start (+) Duration	1st April (+) 15 days = 16th April
Earliest Start	=	Earliest Finish (-) duration	16th April (-) 15 days = 1st April
Latest Start	=	Latest Finish (-) Duration	1st June (-) 15 days = 15th May
Latest Finish	=	Latest Start (+) duration	15th May (+) 15 days = 30th May
Total Float	=	Latest Finish (-) Earliest Finish or Latest Start (-) Earliest Start	1st June (-) 1st June = 45 days 15th May (-) 1st April = 45 days
Free Float	=	Earliest Start of the next activity (-) Earliest Finish of the current activity	

The sum of all the logical relationships of all the activities that make up the project is referred to as the NETWORK DIAGRAM

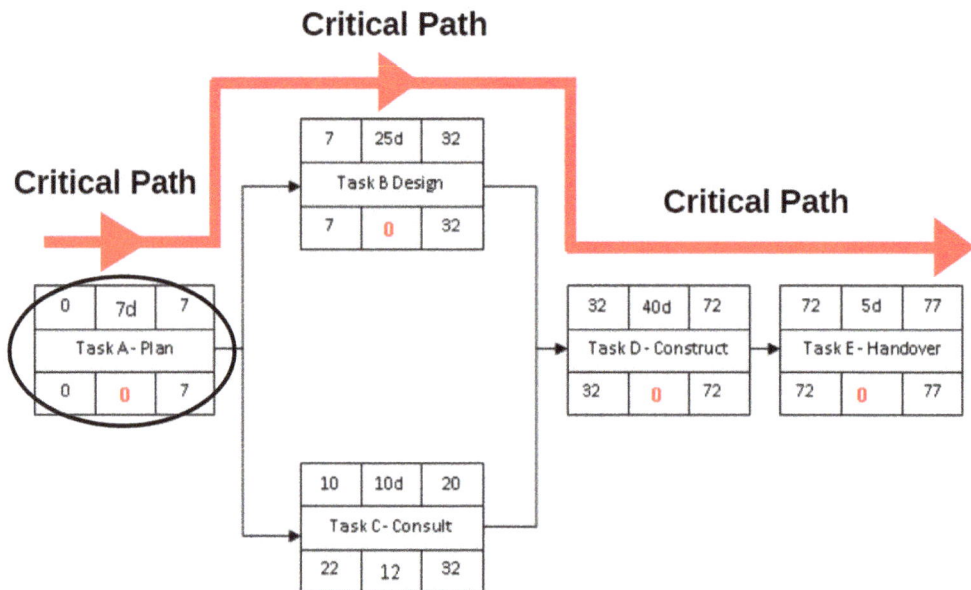

Figure 12.3 Project critical path illustration

In the network diagram above, using the **Task A (Plan)** as an example, the following information can be determined from the activity diagram:

Day 0	7 days	Day 7
Task ID		
Day 0	0 days	Day 7

Earliest Start (ES)	Duration	Earliest Finish (EF)
Task ID		
Latest Start (LS)	Total Float (TF)	Latest Finish (LF)

Duration	7 days
Earliest start	Day 0
Earliest finish	Day 7
Latest start	Day 0
Latest finish	Day 7

Example 2

You are managing a small project to refurbish your kitchen. You have scheduled the things to do in this order:

Day 1	Dismantle existing cabinets Isolate all electrics Clear whole kitchen
Day 2	Rewire the whole kitchen Complete all electrical works and fixings
Day 3	Paint all walls
Day 4	Fit new cabinets Fit new extractor
Day 5	Install new flooring and white goods Hand over

The example above can be used to explain the terminologies:

– **total float, free float, critical path, earliest start** and **latest start**

12.4 Total float

Total float is the amount of time a task or activity can be delayed, rescheduled or extended without affecting the total project duration (end date).

✓ In the example above, assume the electrical contractor booked for day 2 is delayed by up to half a day.
✓ This will mean the scheduled rewiring work may delay and possibly extend to the following day.
✓ This will subsequently have a knock-on effect on the other days' activities and so on, leading to an extension of the completion day to, say, day 6.
✓ However, it is also possible for the various activities to be adjusted such that the overall completion date stays the same.
✓ This is an example of TOTAL FLOAT, where the rewiring has been delayed but did not affect the overall project end date.

12.5 Free float

Free float is the amount of time a task or activity can be delayed, rescheduled, or extended without delaying the start of the succeeding activity.

✓ Using the delay experienced by the electrical contractor on day 2, work as the example:

   o The electrical contractor pulls the lost time back by adding more resource to complete the required work without delaying the start of day 3 works
   o Where the delay to the day 2 activities does not affect the start of the day 3 works, illustrates an example of **free float.**
   o In **free float,** an activity can be delayed or extended without delaying the start of the next activity.

12.6 Critical path analysis

Critical path is the series of activities within a network from start to finish that determines the total project duration.

✓ Using the kitchen refurbishment above as an example, the daily activities can be packed back to back with no possibility of extending or delaying any of them.

✓ In such instances we can say that activities from day 1 to day 5 are on the **critical path** because none can be delayed without subsequently delaying the whole project.

✓ The critical path is also the sum of the longest duration for each activity (to-do item) through the network – similar to taking the worst-case approach.

✓ All projects have a critical path, and it is also possible to have more than one critical path for a project.

✓ Sometimes, activities may need to be delayed or may take longer for one reason or another. As described above, some of these delays can affect the immediate activities that follow; however, the project can recover the time lost such that the agreed end date is kept.

✓ It is not always the case that a delay to an activity will affect the final project end date.

✓ In some situations, delaying activities will have an impact on subsequent activities in a way that the project cannot recover, leading to an overall project delay.

✓ The best way to work out the critical path is to first work out which activities along the network **do not** have any float.

	Week 1	Week 2	Week 3	Week 4	Week 5	Week 6	Week 7	Week 8	Week 9
Task A - Plan									
Task B - Design									
Task C - Consult				Float					
Task D - Construct									
Task E - Handover									

Figure 12.4 Project critical path illustration

In the example above, tasks **A, B, D** and **E** are on the **critical path,** which means any delay to any of the activities will shift the end date into week 10.

Task C has a one week float, which means it can be delayed or extended for up to one week without affecting the project end date or the start of task D.

12.6.1 Why the critical path is useful in project delivery

✓ It helps the project manager to focus attention on specific activities which could delay the project if allowed to slip.
✓ It helps to identify activities with little/no float.
✓ It helps identify when the project manager can manipulate or switch resources between activities with little float and those with large floats.
✓ If any of the activities on the critical path is allowed to slip, the whole project will be delayed.

12.7 The project milestone

We all use milestones in our day-to-day lives, sometimes without even realising this to be the case. We can say milestones are very important dates when certain things or events happen or are expected to happen.

For example, the day you got married, your graduation day, the first time you became a homeowner, when you became a grandad/mum for the first time – these are all important milestones.

> **A milestone** is an important event or date in the project

Projects likewise can have milestones which can be described as important dates when certain events happen on the project.

When managing projects, specific important events can be expected to happen at key points during the delivery. These are the milestones.

12.7.1 Benefits of milestones

✓ They focus the project team towards the project delivery, as well as motivating them
✓ They help to predict if the project delivery is on track or not
✓ They are used to determine important events during the project delivery

12.8 Timeboxing

Timeboxing – commonly used in the interative life cycle approach. Project iterations are fixed to an end date which is not allowed to change. This ensures iterations do not result in project delays.

Timeboxing is a technique used to manage time by allocating a block of time for certain activities. An example of timeboxing may be to allocate, say, three months to complete the project feasibility study. Timeboxing in a project usually fixes the end date when activities should finish, which then forces the project to be delivered to that end date regardless of the number of iterations. It is particularly useful in iterative life cycles where several iterations are developed. Without timeboxing such activities, there is the likelihood of delaying or exceeding the project time allocation.

12.9 The Gantt chart

✓ The commonest way to show the project schedule is to use a Gantt chart (bar chart). This is a graphical representation of activities against time.
✓ You could also use a simple spreadsheet or specialised computer software such as Microsoft Project or Primavera to create a more detailed schedule.
✓ At this basic level, you will be introduced to a simple Gantt chart. This shows the activities (to-do list), as identified in the work breakdown structure, listed vertically on one side, including their duration and expected start date.
✓ Horizontally against each activity/deliverable will be days, weeks or months, whichever will be best used to represent the activity durations.
✓ The Gantt chart displays visual information about the project activities as bars. This makes the project activities easy to follow and understand.

Task ID		Duration	Week 1	Week 2	Week 3	Week 4	Week 5	Week 6	Week 6	Week 7	Week 8
1	Prepare/submit business case	1 week									
2	Business case approval	1 week									
3	Recruit team members	2 weeks								Float	
4	Prepare and obtain approval for the PMP	1 week									
5	Mobilise to start project	1 week									
6	Site set-up	0.5 week									
7	Project commences	4 weeks									
8	Completion and handover	1 week									
9	Clear site										

Figure 12.5 Simple project schedule illustration

Summary

Having read this chapter you should now be aware of and able to:

- State the purpose of scheduling
- State the purpose of critical path analysis
- State the purpose of milestones
- Define the term 'timeboxing'

End-of-chapter assessment – scheduling

Exercise 1 – The humanitarian mission project

> a. Make a list of all the work activities (things to do) on the project. You can copy from the work breakdown structure.
>
> b. Prepare a Gantt chart or bar chart using the 'things to do' and their corresponding durations.

Exercise 2 – The humanitarian mission project

1　Scheduling can best be defined as:

   A. The process for developing, maintaining and communicating schedules for time and resource

   B. The technique the project manager uses to predict when the project activities can start and finish

   C. The building blocks for arranging projects for optimum performance

   D. The process for developing, maintaining and communicating schedules for time

2　Which of the following cannot be classed as one of the approaches to project scheduling?

   A. Gantt chart (bar chart)

   B. Baseline

   C. Milestone

   D. Time

3　Total float can be explained as:

   A. The amount of time an activity can be delayed or extended without affecting the overall duration of the project

   B. The amount of time an activity can be delayed or extended without affecting the duration of the next activity

   C. The total amount of time the project manager can float the deliverables

   D. The value of an organisation's assets floated on the stock market

4   **Free float can be explained as:**

A. The amount of time an activity can be delayed or extended without affecting the overall duration of the project

B. The amount of time an activity can be delayed or extended without affecting the duration of the next activity

C. The total amount of time the project manager can float the deliverables

D. The value of an organisation's assets floated on the stock market

5   **The project critical path can be used to determine:**

A. The critical path the project may follow

B. The critical resources required for project delivery

C. The overall project duration

D. The critical path the project manager should avoid

6   **Which one of these is not a key benefit of using the critical path?**

A. Helps the project manager to focus attention on specific activities which could delay the project if allowed to slip

B. Helps to identify activities with little or no float

C. Helps the project manager to determine the longest path in the project network

D. Helps the project manager to deal with project issues

7   **Which one of the following characteristics applies to a project milestone?**

A. It can be easily exchanged

B. It has a specified duration

C. It represents a collection of activities

D. It represents a key event in the project schedule

8   **Which one of the following best defines a project baseline?**

A. It is the reference point for measuring project costs, time, etc.

B. It is the reference point used by the project manager to determine completion

C. It is the reference point for determining when the project will start

D. It is the reference point for project date and time only

9   **Timeboxing is mainly used in which project life cycle?**

A. Linear project life cycle

B. Iterative project life cycle

C. Extended project life cycle

D. Hybrid project life cycle

10   **Timeboxing is used in project management to:**

A. Extend the activities timeline to ensure the project is not delayed

B. Put project activities in a box to know when they are completed

C. Control time and ensure activities end by a specific time period

D. A and C are correct

CHAPTER 13

HOW TO PROMOTE PROJECT SUCCESS

By the end of this chapter you should be able to:

- Explain success criteria and give examples

- Explain key performance indicators

- Explain success factors

- Differentiate between success factors and critical success factors

- Explain why establishing success criteria is important at the start, during and at the handover of a project

13.1 What does a successful project mean to you?

> **Success criteria** is the yardstick used to determine the clients, users, customers, and stakeholders' requirements have been met.

Success can mean different things to different people. This is because our interpretations of success are rarely the same.

More importantly, what one person may interpret as a successful project, another may not. It's all down to individual views, expectations or, more importantly, the criteria for measuring success.

As a project manager, one of your main objectives is to deliver successful projects. A project may not be judged successful because you delivered quality, on time or within budget. A project is only successful because you met the **agreed success criteria**.

What is the point in delivering a project for a customer or user if in the end their interpretation of success is different from yours?

For example, if the agreed success criteria for the *humanitarian project* is based on providing temporary accommodation for a minimum of 200 people within the agreed budget and time constraints, anything short of this will mean the project has not been successful because the **success criteria** were not met.

Success criteria can be linked to budget, programme, quality, etc.

13.2 Understanding project success factors

> **Success factors** are the necessary conditions, practices, and environment essential for the project to be successful.

All the conditions present within the project environment e.g. within the organisation, that make it possible for the project to be delivered successfully or perform effectively. For example, good leadership, availability of resources, clearly defined processes, experienced staff, etc.

Critical Success Factors are those factors that are deemed essential for the project to be successful. Examples of these factors are;

☐   Clear project goals and objectives
☐   Proper governance structure
☐   Availability of resources
☐   Accurate estimating techniques

All the individual success factors that an organisation adopts collectively form the project delivery culture within the organisation and subsequently become the basis for project performance and success.

13.3 Monitoring success during implementation (key performance indicators (KPIs)

> **Project key performance indicators (KPIs)** are specific measures the project will use to determine if the project is meeting or is likely to meet its planned objectives. KPI is used to determine how well the project is performing towards a successful end.

Key performance indicators can be likened to using signs, observations and indicators to predict how your project could end up or how the project work is performing. A milestone is an example of a key performance indicator. Other examples of key performance indicators include:

–   The amount of money spent at specific intervals versus what was forecasted (example: half of the budget should have been spent by month nine)
–   How the project is performing against the schedule
–   How the project is performing against time
–   Quality expectations

It is one thing agreeing the project deliverables and success criteria, another monitoring the progress at regular intervals to ensure that the project is progressing as planned and that the success criteria will be met.

Projects require constant monitoring during delivery to guarantee that success can be realised. One way of monitoring is by incorporating various measures along the way to indicate that the project is still on track. No one wants disappointments, and certainly these are not welcome in project management. If a project is not going to meet a key deliverable or milestone, it is better to know and prepare or take steps to mitigate this than to be kept in the dark and not know about it.

Key performance indicators are often derived from the **project success criteria.**

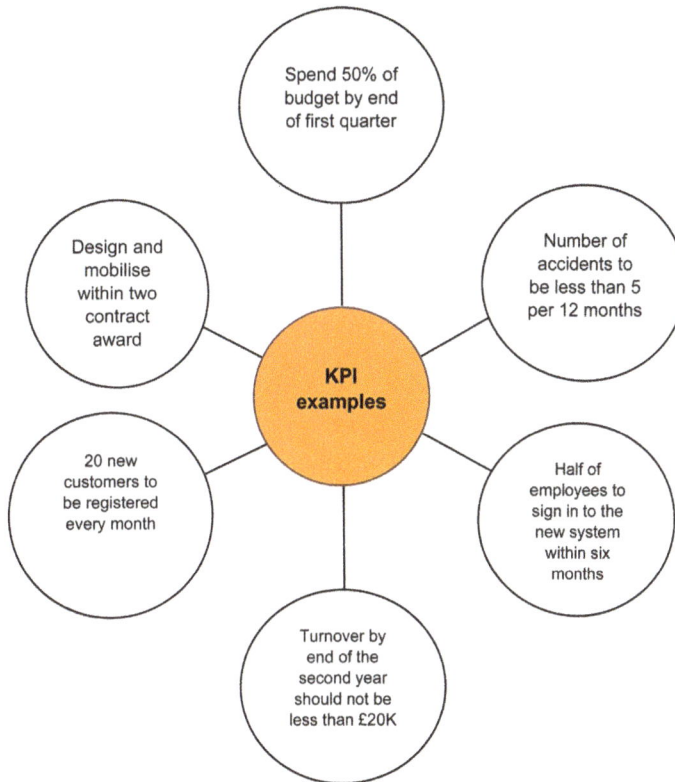

Figure 13.1 Key performance indicators (KPI) examples

Summary

Having read this chapter you should now be aware of and able to:

- Explain success criteria and give examples
- Explain key performance indicators
- Explain success factors
- Differentiate between success factors and critical success factors
- Explain why establishing success criteria is important at the start, during and at the handover of a project

End-of-chapter assessment – how to promote project success

Exercise 1 – The humanitarian mission project

Using the case study topic of the humanitarian mission project,

a. Identify the key performance indicators you will use to predict if the project is progressing according to plan, e.g. by the end of month one, 20% of the budget should have been legitimately spent

b. List five success criteria you will use on completion of the project to measure/determine if the project has been successfully delivered or not

c. What are some of the factors you will consider as critical to the success of this mission? These are the critical success factors without which the mission will fail.

Exercise 2 – The humanitarian mission project

1   **A key performance indicator is best explained as:**

A. Performances which are key to the success of the project

B. The indicators of good performance

C. Measures of success used throughout the project to predict if it is progressing towards the expected end

D. Measuring project factors used to determine if the project will be successful in the end

2   **A key performance indicator will:**

A. Provide assurance if the project is progressing according to plan

B. Boost the performance of the team

C. Ensure the project manager keeps his job

D. Indicate to the sponsor if the project can end

3   **Which of the following cannot be a measure of a project's success?**

A. Clear project goals

B. Availability of funding

C. Availability of resource

D. Availability of young project managers

4   **Which of the following is not a benefit of project success criteria?**

A. Ensures a common agreement of success

B. Removes confusion over whether a project is successful or not

C. Helps to provide clarity and remove assumptions

D. Ensures the project manager's bonus is not missed

5   **Which of the following may not be a critical success factor?**

A. Clear processes for managing projects

B. Availability of laptops for project reporting

C. Availability of experienced project managers

D. Leadership for managing projects

CHAPTER 14

UNDERSTANDING ESTIMATING

By the end of this chapter you should be able to:

- Explain estimating
- Explain why estimates are important when managing projects
- Explain the different estimating techniques
- State typical estimating methods (including analytical, analogous, parametric)
- Outline the purpose of the estimating funnel
- Explain the relationship between the estimating funnel and project phases
- Explain why estimates can be better and more accurate as the project progresses through the life cycle stages

14.1 Estimating

> **Estimate** is the approximation of how much a project, activity, or work will cost or how long it will take to complete.

One day, I invited a contractor to assess a piece of work I needed done. After the contractor's initial visit, my immediate question was: **"How much is this work likely to cost?"** I did not wait for the contractor to carry out a proper assessment or measurement, yet I was expecting him to come up with a cost estimate based on his knowledge and previous experience.

I guess this scenario sounds very familiar. Sometimes, we are asked to provide an estimate, or we ask for an estimate even when the available information to base this on is limited.

Estimates can vary widely from the most likely cost or time outcome. They are affected by the information available at the time of making the estimates. Estimates tend to be more accurate and realistic as the project progresses through the life cycle stages when realistic and accurate information on the project becomes available.

Your ability to estimate accurately will be influenced by several factors, including:

–   Previous experience
–   Perception
–   State of mind and feeling
–   Availability of and access to both previous and current data
–   Life cycle stage

In projects, it often happens that stakeholders, customers and clients may require an estimate of costs and timescales to assist with decision-making. Depending on when the estimates are provided (which life cycle stage), they could have very wide variation from the most likely cost and time outcomes.

Therefore, there is a need to understand estimating techniques to support accurate estimating. An estimate at the very early stages of the project will vary widely from estimates made at the later stages of the same project.

14.2 Estimating funnel

Where project estimates narrow and become more accurate as the project progress through the life cycle stages. This is referred to as the **ESTIMATING FUNNEL** (because the estimate narrows from concept to closeout, taking the shape of a funnel).

The estimating funnel explains the fact that estimates with wide variation narrow as the project progresses through the life cycle and more information becomes available or the scope is better understood.

Although estimates are not intended to be perfect, they must represent a good educated guess. They are expected to be realistic and not too far from the most likely scenario.

Estimates should not be based on feelings or wild guesses. Adopting a tried and tested estimating approach or technique is always the best approach.

Always relying on your feeling rather than the tried and tested approach is a poor estimating technique.

Various approaches can be used to estimate project cost and time.

Estimating funnel

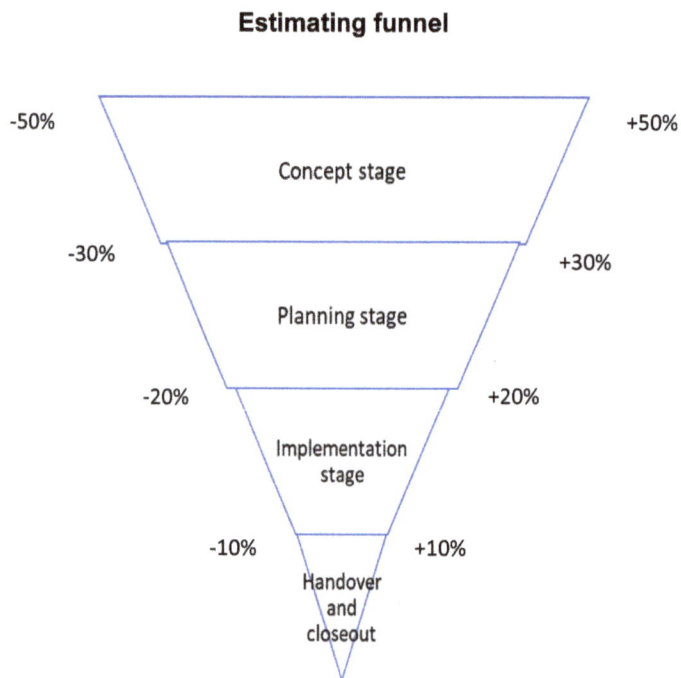

Figure 14.1 Estimating funnel illustration

Estimating is the use of different methods, approaches, and techniques to approximate the project cost and time.

14.3 Estimating techniques

Table 14.1 Estimating techniques

Estimating technique	Description
Bottom-up approach	✓ This approach makes use of the work breakdown structure by adding the individual costs and time estimates to provide an informed overall estimate of cost and duration for the project. ✓ An understanding of the full work breakdown structure is key to this estimating technique. Example: if there are four separate activities that must be completed for a project and each takes two days to complete, as per the WBS, it implies that the overall project will take eight days to complete. This will be our educated guess.
Analogous approach	✓ With this technique, you compare the cost of similar projects or activities in the past and scale it up or down to reflect the project in question. ✓ Previous experience and knowledge of the cost and schedule of similar projects is fundamental to this approach.
Parametric approach	✓ This technique uses data of itemised or unit costs and rates to multiply with the quantities required. ✓ An example is multiplying the known hourly rate by the total number of hours required.

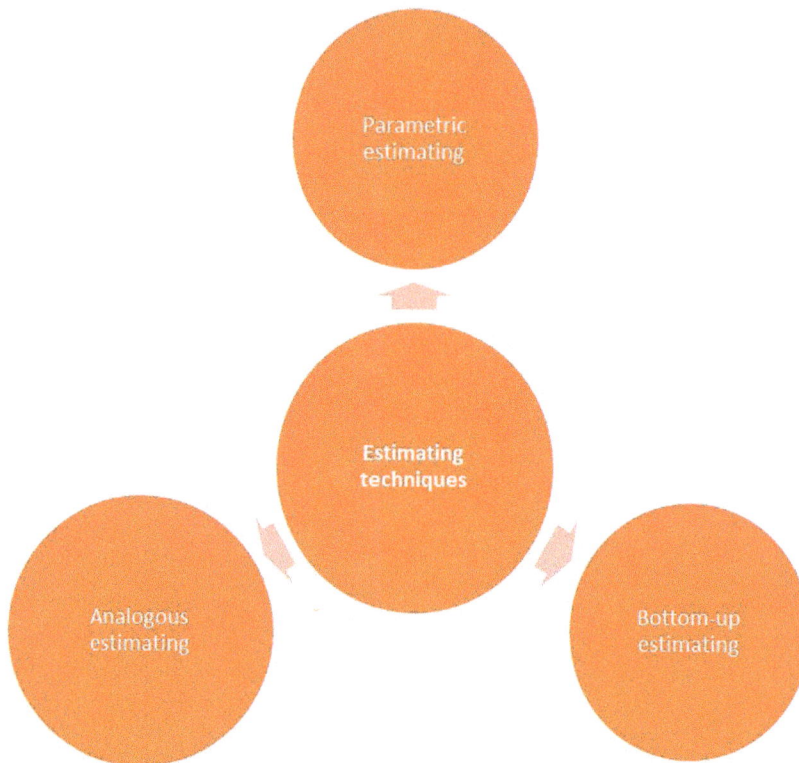

Figure 14.2 Estimating techniques

Summary

Having read this chapter you should now be aware of and able to:

– Explain estimating
– Explain why estimates are important when managing projects
– Explain the different estimating techniques
– State typical estimating methods (including analytical, analogous, parametric)
– Outline the purpose of the estimating funnel
– Explain the relationship between the estimating funnel and project phases
– Explain why estimates can be better and more accurate as the project progresses through the life cycle stages

End-of-chapter assessment

Exercise 1 – The humanitarian mission project

Using the case study topic of the **humanitarian mission**, imagine that you must estimate the cost of the mission for inclusion in the business case. How will you go about preparing a best estimate, and which estimating method can you use and why?

Exercise 2 – The humanitarian mission project

1   **Estimation is best explained as:**

   A. The prediction of a project's cost

   B. The prediction of a project's time

   C. An educated guess of a project's cost and time

   D. An estimated guess of a project's cost, time and quality

2   **A bottom-up estimating technique involves:**

   A. Making use of the work breakdown structure to sum up the individual estimates of cost and time

   B. Any estimates that start from the bottom to the top

   C. An estimate which makes use of only the bottom numbers

   D. All of the above

3   **A parametric estimating technique:**

   A. Makes use of different parameters to estimate

   B. Is a type of estimate that is based on parametric

   C. Makes use of itemised unit costs and rates to multiply with the quantities required

   D. Is a type of estimate similar to what paramedics use

4   **Which is true about the analogous estimating technique?**

    A. Compares all estimates from previous years

    B. Compares two estimates to help decide on the best one

    C. Compares previous estimates from similar projects which are then scaled up or down

    D. Compares the project manager's estimate with the supplier's estimate

5   **Which of the following does not impact on one's ability to estimate accurately?**

    A. Previous experience

    B. Race

    C. Project life cycle stage

    D. Availability of data

6   **The term 'estimating funnel' is used because:**

    A. Estimates can be filtered through a funnel

    B. Estimates are used to filter costs

    C. Estimates narrow as the project progresses through the life cycle

    D. B and C are correct

CHAPTER 15

UNDERSTANDING CONFIGURATION

By the end of this chapter you should be able to:

– Define the term 'configuration management'

– List the steps involved in managing the configuration of a product

– Outline the activities in a typical configuration management process (including planning, identification, control, status accounting and verification audit)

– Explain the relationship between change control and configuration management

15.1 Configuration management

'**Configuration management** encompasses the technical and administrative activities concerned with the creation, maintenance, controlled change and quality control of the scope of work' - (Murray-Webster, Dalcher and Association for Project Management, 2019).

Configuration management can be explained as all the administrative work that is needed to provide **unique identities** for the various parts of a project, e.g. drawings, components or the product itself.

Have you considered how many individual parts/components there may be in a computer, phone, car, aircraft, etc.? There will probably be thousands, with each tiny part playing a crucial role in how the overall product functions.

During the life of any project, different versions of components, drawings, products, designs, parts, etc. may be produced every time **changes** are agreed.

What if these **changes** are not reflected in the latest versions, or controlled to allow clear distinction between superseded and latest versions? It can be catastrophic to build a permanent structure or mass produce products based on the wrong version of critical components because changes in earlier versions were not captured and incorporated in later versions.

It may be costly and risky to introduce an out-of-date product or component which looks the same in appearance as a newer version. These scenarios described above form the basis of **CONFIGURATION MANAGEMENT.** They are more than version control for products and drawings.

15.2 Configuration and change control

–   Configuration and change control are closely linked to each other; a change can affect the other. For example, changing the design of a product can affect several configuration items related to the design
–   Together, configuration and change processes ensure that project deliverables meet the required specifications
–   Configuration can be applied to key project management documents like the business case and the PMP through simple version control

    – The project team will usually be best placed to ensure all project configuration management plans are implemented.

15.3 Configuration management process

Configuration management follows five distinct steps:

1. Planning
2. Identification
3. Controlling
4. Status accounting
5. Verification/auditing

Table 15.1 Configuration management process

Configuration planning	A configuration management plan - describes all procedures, processes, and applications during the project delivery. The plan also identifies roles and responsibilities during the configuration management process.
Configuration identification	The project or product components are broken down into deliverables (configuration items). Unique identification numbers or references are assigned to each configuration item. These will become the baseline (reference) point for the configuration items and tracked throughout the project as changes occur.
Configuration controlling	Through controlling, all identified configuration items are documented and maintained. This is where the linkages between the configuration items are also identified and controlled. The controlling stage ensures that all changes to configuration items are captured and documented.
Configuration status accounting	The status of a configuration item is tracked throughout the project. This ensures changes to each identified configuration can be tracked throughout the project.

Configuration verification and auditing	All configuration items must be verified and audited to determine whether the deliverables conform to the original requirements and configuration information on project completion. An example of configuration auditing could be physical observation to determine conformity to the product specification. Other forms of auditing could be functional to check that those configuration items perform the function for which they were designed. Another type of audit could check that the configuration management system is working effectively.

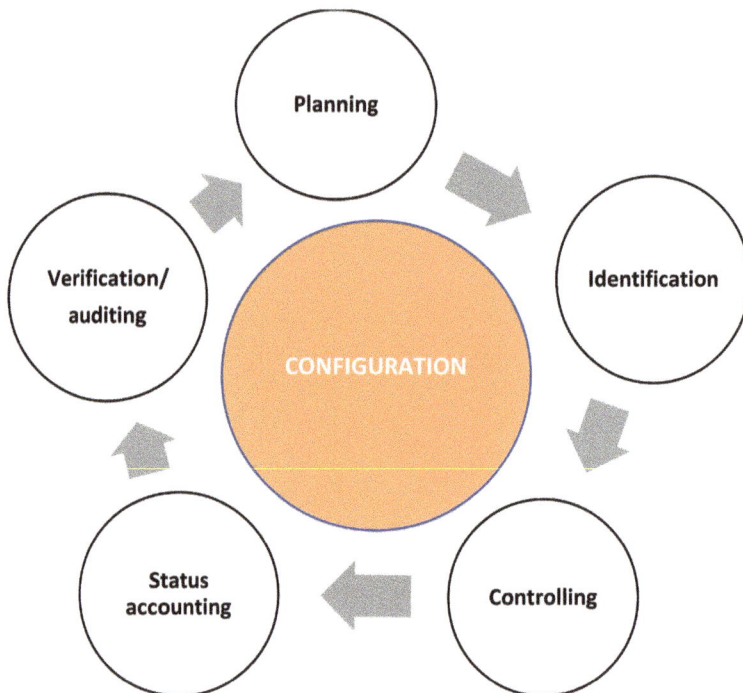

Figure 15.1 Configuration management steps

Summary

Having read this chapter you should now be aware of and able to:

–   Define the term 'configuration management'
–   List the steps involved in managing the configuration of a product
–   Outline the activities in a typical configuration management process (including planning, identification, control, status accounting and verification audit)
–   Explain the relationship between change control and configuration management

End-of-chapter assessment – configuration

Exercise 1 – The humanitarian mission project

1. **Which of the following will not be a typical configuration management activity?**
   A. Administrative work required to provide unique identities for products
   B. Identifying the interrelationship between configuration items
   C. Tracing changes in a configuration item throughout its development
   D. Configuration activities carried out by the project manager and sponsor

2. **A typical configuration management process follows this sequence:**
   A. Planning, identification, controlling, status accounting, verification/auditing
   B. Planning, recording, reference allocation and documenting
   C. Version control, recording, updating and verification
   D. Identification, planning, controlling, verification/auditing

3. **Verification during configuration management helps with:**
   A. Determining whether a deliverable conforms to its requirements
   B. Verifying the physical characteristics of the deliverable for conformity
   C. Checking whether all the necessary test documentations have been completed
   D. Tracking the current status of configuration items

4. **Changes and configuration are closely linked:**
   A. True
   B. False

5. **Which of these may not be a benefit of adopting configuration management?**
   A. Changes in products, drawings and items can be tracked
   B. Can save cost in the long run
   C. Helps avoid reputational damage
   D. Helps to develop aesthetically pleasing products

CHAPTER 16

DEALING WITH CHANGES

By the end of this chapter you should be able to:

- Define the term 'change'
- Explain what is meant by 'change control'
- Explain what goes into a typical change control process
- Explain how changes affect project scope
- Understand who is responsible for managing changes

16.1 Change control

In project management, a deviation from the project **baseline** (see chapter eight) in terms of scope, cost, time and quality objectives will imply a **change**. In projects, changes must be closely monitored and assessed each time they occur on a project for their impact.

The reason for this is that changes on a project can have a catastrophic impact on what and how a project is delivered if not properly managed. A formal change control will be used to manage and control project changes as they occur.

> '**Change control** is the process through which all requests to change the approved baseline of a project, programme or portfolio are captured, evaluated and then approved, rejected or deferred' - (Murray-Webster, Dalcher and Association for Project Management, 2019).

Change management is the formal process through which changes to the project plans are approved and introduced.

As the project progresses, you must remember that changes may be required because they are inevitable on projects. As the project manager, you must be aware of and understand what to do when changes occur or are required. This is when the change control process as planned is put into practical use.

The project manager must follow the change control process in order to be in good stead to steer and control the project to an expected end.

A typical change control process will capture at least the following information:

- change requestor details
- description of the change
- known impact of the change (time, cost, quality, risks, success criteria, etc.)

16.1.1 How changes affect the project scope

✓ In project delivery, it is not uncommon for **changes** to be requested by the client, customers, stakeholders or users at any point in time in the project delivery stage. In other words, any project member can request a change to any aspect of a project; however, whether this change is included or not is another matter.
✓ How changes are agreed and incorporated into the project, especially after all the plans have been agreed, baselined and implementation is in progress, can all be controlled.

✓ The **change control process** acts as the gateway for controlling how changes are incorporated into the project, rejected or deferred.

✓ Every change has the potential to impact negatively or positively on the project delivery time, cost, quality, success criteria and risk.

✓ Changes during project delivery are inevitable – some may be justified and legitimate, others may just be wishes and desires.

✓ There are several ways and instances where changes can be requested. It can be via a telephone conversation, an email, at a meeting or in a face-to-face conversation. Changes in legislation can also affect the project, etc.

✓ It is advisable for the project manager to create and use a change form to capture key information from the initial change request. This will be your first step to controlling and monitoring project changes.

16.2 Change control and configuration

✓ All project changes must be reviewed for their impact on project cost, time, quality and scope, etc.

✓ Project changes must also be reviewed in line with the identified project configuration items before incorporating into the project.

✓ Sometimes a change to one part or component may require this to be reviewed against the configuration items to see if any update is required.

✓ For example, a change to the dimension of a door opening may require, for example, the relevant drawings to be updated to show the new door size.

✓ Other configuration items should also be reviewed for impact; for example, changing the dimension of a door opening may require the door size to also change in line with the new dimension.

✓ Other elements of the building linked to the door may also need to be updated if they are configuration items.

✓ Whenever a change to any aspect of a project is agreed, this should be checked with relevant configuration items and updated accordingly.

✓ Not linking project changes to configuration items may result in mistakes and expensive rework or the introduction of unauthorised project components, etc.

16.3 Change control responsibilities

✓ Usually the project sponsor has the overall responsibility for approving project changes when they exceed the project manager's delegated authority.

✓ The sponsor may delegate smaller change approvals to the project manager and only approve major project changes.

✓ Sometimes, when change approval is above the sponsor's delegated authority, it can be escalated to the next level of authorisation for approval.

16.4 The project manager and change control

✓ The project manager is responsible for implementing a change control procedure.
✓ The project manager must ensure the process is understood by every team member.
✓ The project manager must monitor the change evaluation and the implementation process.

16.5 Change control process

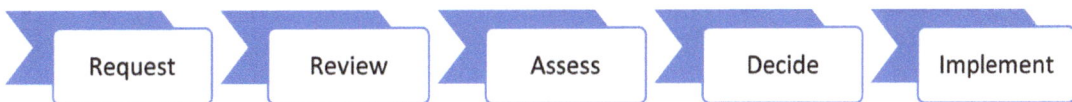

| Request | Review | Assess | Decide | Implement |

Figure 16.1 The change control process

Request	Changes to any project aspect can be requested by anyone involved in the project, stakeholders, team, users. The project manager gathers sufficient high-level information about the change and document in the change register at the request stage.
Review	At this stage, the project manager carries out a high-level review of the change request to determine any impact on the project objectives, timescale, quality, cost. Should it be deemed necessary to assess the change further, the change will progress to the next stage. If not, the proposed change will be accepted, rejected, or deferred by the project manager with reasons.
Assessment	At the assessment stage, a change request will undergo a detailed evaluation to determine the full impact on the project cost, time, quality, objectives, etc. Once the thorough assessment is carried out, a decision will be made to accept, reject, or defer the change.
Decision	Change decisions are always communicated to the requestor and the team as per the communication plan. Sometimes approves changes impact on the project configuration, which also means the relevant teams in charge of project configuration should also be informed.

| Implementation | Before implementing approved project changes, relevant plans, drawings, and configuration items should be changed. Change control and configuration management are closely linked to each other. Most likely, a change to an aspect of the project can affect a configuration item. |

Summary

Having read this chapter you should now be aware of and able to:

– Define the term 'change'
– Explain what is meant by 'change control'
– Explain what goes into a typical change control process
– Explain how changes affect project scope
– Understand who is responsible for managing changes

End-of-chapter assessment – dealing with changes

Exercise 1 – The humanitarian mission project

There is a new request to change the number of accommodation stock and provide 20% additional accommodation over and above what has been agreed. Can you analyse this change and present the impact to the project board/sponsor for approval?

Exercise 2 – The humanitarian mission project

1　**Project changes should be controlled because:**

　　A.　Every change costs money

　　B.　Uncontrolled changes can be catastrophic to the project

　　C.　Changes usually happen just before handover

　　D.　The project management plan says so

2　**Which of the following is not one of the change control steps:**

　　A.　Change request

　　B.　Change review

　　C.　Change assessment

　　D.　Change acceptance

3　**The change control process acts as:**

　　A.　A unique process the project manager uses

　　B.　A gate for controlling how changes are included or rejected

　　C.　The project manager's weapon for changing the project

　　D.　A tool for managing successful projects

4　**Who is responsible for managing the project change control process?**

　　A.　The organisation that owns the project

　　B.　The senior leadership teams

　　C.　The project manager

　　D.　The project sponsor

5   **This is what happens during the 'review' stage of the change control process:**

A. A detailed review of the change is carried out for its impact

B. A high-level review of the change is carried out for its impact

C. Experts are asked to review the change and comment

D. All of the above

6   **Who is responsible for ensuring the change control process is understood by all?**

A. The project management office

B. The team leader

C. The project manager

D. The project sponsor

7   **Who usually makes the decision on project changes?**

A. The project team

B. The project sponsor

C. The project manager

D. Anyone

8   **Which of the following is one of the activities during a change control process?**

A. Escalation

B. Assessment

C. Recommendation

D. Planning

9   **Following a change control process, which of the following must happen as part of rigorous configuration management?**

A. Costs associated with the change are evaluated and documented.

B. Risks associated with the change are monitored to avoid delays to the project.

C. The item is approved or declined in line with stakeholder expectations.

D. Documents are updated to include any approved changes.

CHAPTER 17

MANAGING RESOURCES

By the end of this chapter you should be able to:

- Explain 'project resources' and 'resource management'
- Understand the types of resources and give examples
- Understand the techniques used in managing resources
- Explain resource levelling and resource smoothing

17.1 Project resource management

✓ Projects are delivered by people, with materials/equipment, knowledge and the expense of time. All of these are types of **RESOURCES** required to deliver the project.

> **Resource management** is the process by which all the required resources needed for the project are acquired internally or externally and used on the project.

✓ There is no benefit to planning a project when the resources will not be available to deliver the project.
✓ Also, the appropriate management and use of resources at the optimum level not only ensures successful project delivery but efficient and effective use of the project budget.
✓ There are many techniques that can be deployed to manage project resources. For example, there may be instances where resources become limited, unavailable or scarce, and balancing and distributing the resources to meet the needs of the project will be a skill the project manager must exhibit during project delivery.
✓ No project manager will be given unlimited amounts of resources to deliver projects.
✓ There is always a degree of conflict that exists between project delivery needs and the available resources.
✓ The process of identifying the resources needed and assigning them to activities is called **RESOURCE MANAGEMENT.**

17.2 Types of project resources

The resources needed to deliver a project will include: people, financial resources, machinery, materials, technology, property and anything else required to deliver the work.

Resources may be obtained internally from the host organisation or procured from external sources.

Consumable resources	Consumable resources are typically the materials and components required to complete tasks; for example, paint, carpets, etc. Consumable resources are used up by tasks and are usually not available to be reused on other tasks.
Re-usable resources	Machines People Equipment

17.3 Resource management techniques

When the project resource requirements and their availability are defined, this helps with planning the demands appropriately.

Project resources can effectively be managed through:

- **Allocation** – identifying the resources needed to complete a piece of work (quantity and effort required)
- **Aggregation** – summing up the total resources required per day, week, month, etc.
- **Scheduling** – When the amount/quantity of resources required are calculated

Good resource allocation can be linked to effective project scheduling.

17.4 Resource smoothing (used when time constraints take priority)

This can simply be explained as a process of managing the resources available to you by making use of more/spare resources to cover where there is less or a scarcity.

In summary, the available resources will be efficiently used in a way that keeps the project end date intact.

Resource smoothing is used when time is critical for project completion.

17.5 Resource levelling (used when resource availability takes priority)

This is different from smoothing in that levelling tends to spread the resources and extend the end date as well.

This happens when the project has very limited resources available. For example, only one machine or plant is available instead of two, or only two experienced personnel are available to operate a machine.

With limited resources, the project manager will maximise the use of resources and try to spread them out and not over allocate. This is used especially when the end date is not critical.

Summary

Having read this chapter you should now be aware of and able to:

- Explain 'project resources' and 'resource management'
- Understand the types of resources and give examples
- Understand the techniques used in managing resources
- Explain resource levelling and resource smoothing

End-of-chapter assessment – resource management

Exercise 1 – The humanitarian mission project

Using the case study topic of the humanitarian mission project, list some of the resources you may need for this mission. Group your list into re-usable and consumable resources.

Exercise 2 – The humanitarian mission project

1 Resource management can be defined as:

   A. The acquisition and deployment of internal and external resources required to deliver the project

   B. The management of resources efficiently

   C. The procurement of resources by the project manager

   D. The effective management of resources by the project management

2 Which is an example of a project resource?

   A. Machines

   B. People

   C. Vehicles

   D. All of the above

3 Which of the following is not a re-usable resource?

   A. Land

   B. People

   C. Machines

   D. Fuel

4   **Which of the following is not a resource management technique?**

A. Resource allocation

B. Resource aggregation

C. Resource scheduling

D. Resource speeding

5   **Resource levelling involves:**

A. Spreading the resource because of scarcity

B. Keeping the end date because of resource scarcity

C. Making use of spare resources available to you

D. None of the above

6   **Resource smoothing is used when:**

A. Time constraints are critical

B. Resource availability takes priority

C. Both resource availability and time constraints are critical

D. The project manager wants to save money

7   **Resource levelling is used when:**

A. Time constraints are critical

B. Resource availability takes priority

C. Both resource availability and time constraints are critical

D. The project manager wants to save money

8   **The two categories of resources are:**

A. Consumable and re-usable

B. People and equipment

C. Materials and human resources

D. Machinery and people

CHAPTER 18

PROCUREMENT

By the end of this chapter you should be able to:

– Explain procurement

– Explain the importance of procurement

– Understand what a contract is and when it is appropriate to use

18.1 Procurement

> **Procurement** is how goods, services, or works are sourced from an external party to incorporate or use on the project. Procurement will also involve contract arrangement and execution and managing the relationship with the suppliers.

Projects sometimes require goods and services to be used as part of its delivery. The process that must be followed to ensure the appropriate goods and services that the project needs are acquired from an external provider is termed, as procurement.

Project management becomes less useful if you cannot find and procure the right products and services to implement what you have spent hours, days and years planning. The aspect of project management that deals with procuring the right products and services for integration into the project is procurement. It is fundamental to project success because, regardless of how carefully a project is planned, if poor products and services are procured, the deliverables are likely to be negatively affected, resulting in poor quality, expensive deliverables and/or reworking, delays, etc.

Usually, procurement methods will first be addressed at the strategic level where a procurement strategy that suits the organisation may be set out. For example, some organisations may only procure from a pre-vetted list of suppliers or from a specific source.

The organisation's procurement strategy is further developed and addressed within the project management plan (PMP) to refine how the procurement for a specific project may be undertaken. For example, a project within the organisation may be procured by fully transferring the design risk to a supplier, whereas another may be designed in-house.

Procurement strategy considerations:

✓ Buy off-the-shelf items or make them
✓ Design/produce goods in-house or procure from an external supplier
✓ Seek professional advice/use consultants
✓ Use single, integrated or multiple suppliers
✓ Type of service provider relationship
✓ Selection process
✓ Terms of engagement
✓ Pricing and repayment structure, etc.

Procurement strategy is the high-level and an overarching approach an organisation will use to purchase goods, services or works from external suppliers. The strategy may include a strategy for selecting service providers or managing the relationships.

In summary:

✓ The project management plan (PMP) addresses how goods and services will be procured to meet the project objectives.

✓ Projects do not always need external resources. Sometimes, the team or organisation may choose to make or carry out the work in-house rather than finding and using external contractors, suppliers or service providers.

✓ It is important to carefully select the right suppliers and contractors with the required level of knowledge and experience to do the job.

✓ A careful selection process or criteria should be followed when selecting the preferred supplier, contractor or service provider.

✓ Selecting the right supplier for your project is an important process because it can have a direct impact on the project.

✓ Some organisations will only engage a preferred supplier to provide them with services, while others will use a competitive tendering process in an open market to find suppliers.

✓ Sometimes competitive tendering from a pre-approved list of contractors/suppliers can be used.

18.2 Contract agreements

Contract is a legal agreement made between two or more parties. Contracts are usually legally enforceable and sets out the commitments and responsibilities of the parties involved.

Once the supplier has been selected, and depending on the type of work and the complexity, a formal contract can be agreed between the parties as may be appropriate.

Contracts are legally binding, formal agreements on how the parties will work together in executing the project. Depending on the industry, various standard contract types may be used.

Not all projects require a formal agreement or written contract between the parties involved, particularly if you are doing everything yourself or using internal resources.

There may also come a time when a formal agreement between the parties involved in the project may be necessary for the purpose of executing the project.

The type of contract will usually be decided between the parties involved in the project, but most importantly it will depend on the type of work and the industry.

For instance, a simple job like replacing a kitchen tap in your house may only require a verbal promise and agreement, compared to undertaking a significant project like building a house where a written contract or agreement may be appropriate and will offer better protection for all parties involved.

The agreement/contract will set out what services are being provided and at what cost. Several items may also be included in the contract; for example, specific terms and conditions, payment terms, cancellation of the agreement, arrangement for managing changes, dealing with unforeseen events, payments and conflicts, etc.

Different industries may use different contracts suitable for that industry. Regardless of which industry, it is sensible to ensure an appropriate contract is in place to cover all parties involved.

Summary

Having read this chapter you should now be aware of and able to:

-   Explain procurement
-   Explain the importance of procurement
-   Understand what a contract is and when it is appropriate to use

End-of-chapter assessment – procurement

Exercise 1 – The humanitarian mission project

1 Procurement can be defined as:

   A. The process by which goods and services required for the project are sold

   B. The process by which goods and services required for the project are acquired

   C. The process by which goods and services required for the project are acquired from an external provider

   D. The process by which goods and services required for the project are acquired from an external provider for incorporation into the project

2 Which of the following is not a procurement consideration?

   A. Buy

   B. Make

   C. Sell

   D. All of the above

3 A contract can simply be explained as:

   A. An agreement between two people

   B. An agreement between two or more parties

   C. An agreement between two or more parties that creates a legally binding obligation

   D. An acceptance of an offer to carry out a piece of work

4 Which project document will address how goods and services will be procured to meet the project objectives?

   A. Project management plan

   B. Project procurement plan

   C. Business case

   D. Business strategy

CHAPTER 19

DEALING WITH RISKS

By the end of this chapter you should be able to:

– Define the term 'risk'

– Explain the purpose of risk management

– Outline the stages of a typical risk management process (including identification, analysis, response and closure)

– Describe the use of risk registers

19.1 Risks

> **Risk** is the probability of something happening on the project such that it can affect all or some of the project objectives from being achieved.

Understanding project risks

✓ Projects are by their very nature risky because they involve a change that results in something new and unique.

✓ Every time something new and unique is embarked upon, it can be very difficult to predict what may happen along the way (unknowns) – these could be good or bad events (risks).

✓ Risks are not only the things that can go wrong, they are also the **opportunities** that can be exploited to the advantage of the project. For example the humanitarian mission project can exploit the opportunity to train the locals in disaster response management.

✓ Risks can be associated with project cost, resource, scope changes, health and safety issues, weather and many more. They can also be opportunities that can be exploited by the project.

✓ Risks may come from within the organisation or be external to the organisation.

✓ RISK MANAGEMENT can therefore be explained as the process of identifying, assessing and responding appropriately to project risks.

✓ It is the responsibility of the project manager to take active steps to identify risks, assess their impact on the project and plan appropriate responses to mitigate or exploit them.

✓ There are strategies and steps that can be used to identify, assess and respond to the things that could go wrong or well on a project. This is simply called **RISK MANAGEMENT.**

19.2 When should project risks be identified?

–   As soon as possible in the project
–   On a regular basis throughout the project
–   Consistently, for example, weekly or monthly through a risk workshop
–   Whenever there is a change
–   At certain specific project milestones

> **Risk** management is the process that allows project risks to be proactively identified, analysed, and responded to effectively.

Risk management ensures that project risks are proactively identified, assessed, and managed. The purpose is to give the project the best possible chance of succeeding within the prevailing constraints.

Risk management means foreseeing what could possibly affect the project, either positively or negatively, and taking the necessary steps to manage or mitigate these events such that the project manager can maximise the opportunities or minimise the negative impact (threats).

Managing risk is therefore an **intentional approach** to minimise or eliminate potential project crises and proactively look for opportunities to even do things better. Projects by their nature carry **risks** because they are unique endeavours which can be complex. They may have several unknowns and assumptions which make them risky.

19.3 Risk management process

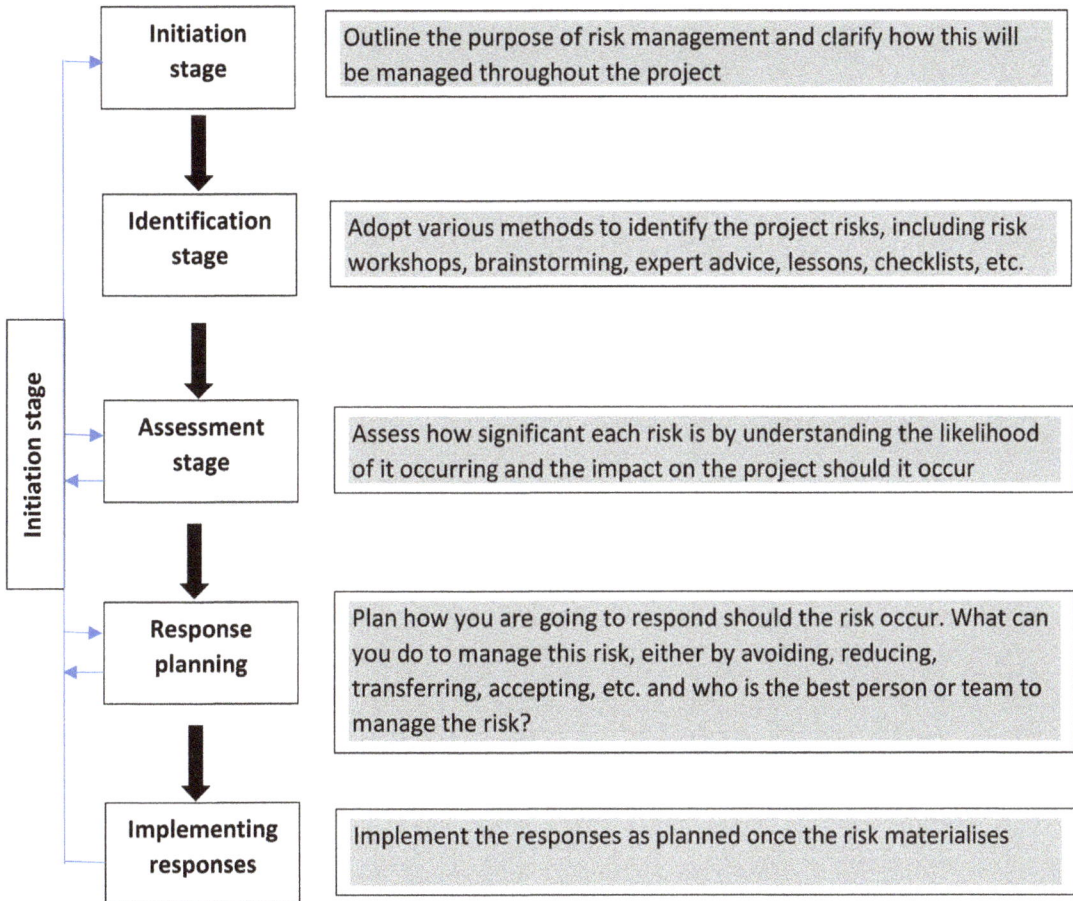

Initiation stage	Outline the purpose of risk management and clarify how this will be managed throughout the project
Identification stage	Adopt various methods to identify the project risks, including risk workshops, brainstorming, expert advice, lessons, checklists, etc.
Assessment stage	Assess how significant each risk is by understanding the likelihood of it occurring and the impact on the project should it occur
Response planning	Plan how you are going to respond should the risk occur. What can you do to manage this risk, either by avoiding, reducing, transferring, accepting, etc. and who is the best person or team to manage the risk?
Implementing responses	Implement the responses as planned once the risk materialises

Figure 19.1 The risk management process

19.4 Risk identification

Risk identification is the proactive process of finding the things that could go wrong or the opportunities that could be exploited for the benefit of the project.

There are different methods and strategies that can be used to identify project risks. Remember that you do not have to solely rely on your own knowledge and experience, rather you should make use of all available risk identification techniques.

19.4.1 Risk identification techniques

Table 19.1 Risk identification techniques

Technique	Description
Brainstorming	A team of individuals, stakeholders, subject matter experts, etc. come together to explore and identify potential risks.
Lessons from previous projects	Lessons from past projects can be a good source for identification of project risks.
Questionnaires	Like prompt lists but in the form of questions that the project manager, team members respond to.
Risk workshops	A risk workshop can be held to bring individuals together to think about project risks, consequences, probabilities, etc.
Delphi method	Subject matter experts are consulted and utilised to generate questions for debate, which the project manager can then discuss with others to form a collaborative response.
Interviews	Another form of discussion or reviewing project risks. This is best when a formal meeting may not be possible.
SWOT analysis	Identification of the project strengths, weaknesses, opportunities and threats.
Prompt lists	Specific risk heading is used to prompt or stimulate thoughts on risk associated with the prompt area.
Checklists	Based on previous risks as identified on similar projects, a checklist is a compiled list of previous or most common risks.

19.5 Risk analysis/assessment

✓ Once risks associated with the project are identified, there is a process for assessing each risk to understand its likelihood and impact on the project.
✓ Analysing each risk will involve a process of approximating how likely you or your team think that each risk will occur and, if they do, what the impact could be on time, cost, quality, reputation, etc.
✓ Sometimes risk analysis could include **risk proximity**; this is a measure of how soon the risk could occur (now, soon, during the implementation stage). Include risk proximity to plan mitigation strategies appropriately.

Risk likelihood and impact scores could be documented as:

Table 19.2 Risk likelihood and impact

Likelihood	Impact
Very likely	Negligible
Likely	Minor
Possible	Moderate
Unlikely	Serious
Very unlikely	Critical

19.6 Risk register

✓ A risk register is simply a list of risks with their associated likelihood of occurrence, probability, mitigation strategy, owner, etc.
✓ A risk register provides more detail and information about each risk.

A typical risk register will have the following headings:

☐ Risk identifier – a unique reference number
☐ Risk description
☐ Risk probability
☐ Risk impact
☐ Risk response – how you will respond or deal with the risk
☐ Risk proximity – how soon or close the risk is
☐ Risk owner – who owns the risk: client, supplier, etc.
☐ Risk status – open, closed, pending

The table below is a much-simplified risk register:

Table 19.3 Risk register example

Risk ID	Risk description	Probability	Impact	Risk owner	Response/ Action	Due date	Status
1							
2							
3							

19.7 Probability impact grid

✓ A risk probability impact grid can be created using the estimated probability and impact from the risk register.
✓ Both probability and impact can be scored between 1 and 5 (with 1 being the lowest and 5 the highest).

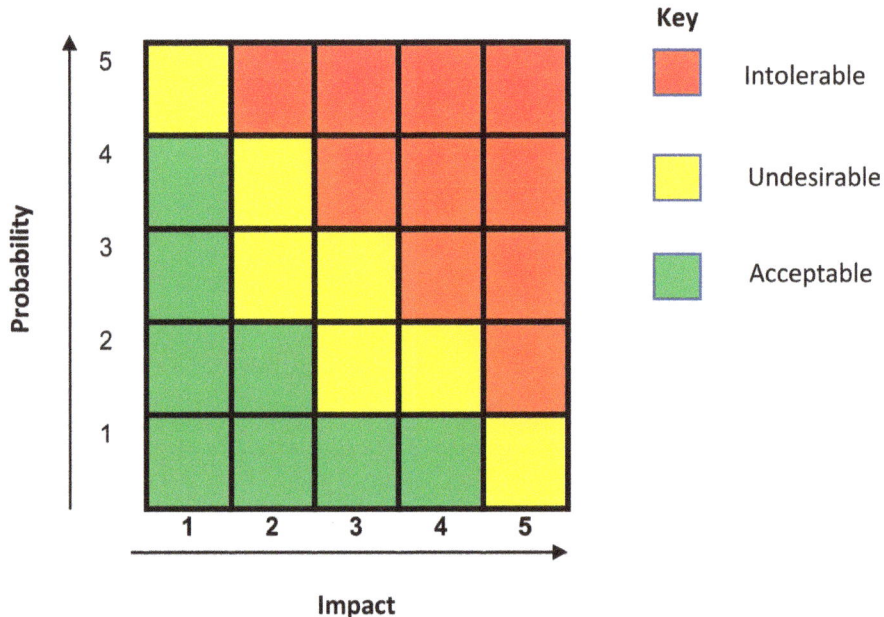

Figure 19.2 Risk probability impact grid

19.8 Responding to risks

✓ The purpose of risk management is to be able to foresee what could possibly happen that can affect the project either positively or negatively.
✓ It also means finding ways to respond appropriately to risks.
✓ If risks occur, the project manager deals with these in accordance with the agreed strategy outlined in the risk management plan.
✓ Responding to project risks could involve spending money, additional resource, changing the time requirement or a change in the project delivery strategy.
✓ For example, if a risk around equipment breaking down occurs, the response could be to purchase new, repair or hire another.
✓ In the pages below, we will review the various options the project manager can use to respond to risks once they occur on the project.

Threats	Opportunities
Avoid – Can you avoid the risk altogether by doing or using something else?	**Exploit** – Can you change something slightly to achieve the maximum benefit from the project? Is there something you can take advantage of because of the project?
Reduce – If you cannot avoid or exploit the risk, can you reduce the impact?	**Enhance** – Can you identify an opportunity to enhance?
Transfer – Can you transfer the risk to another organisation? It may be possible to reduce the financial impact of a risk by buying insurance cover.	**Share** – Is there an opportunity to share the risk with another party so you don't bear it alone?
Accept – Sometimes, having done all you can to avoid, reduce or transfer the risk, your only other option will be to accept the risk and have contingency in place to absorb the risk. Time contingency – allow for time just in case the risk happens.	**Reject** – Sometimes the opportunity of a risk can be rejected because the benefits are not worth pursuing.

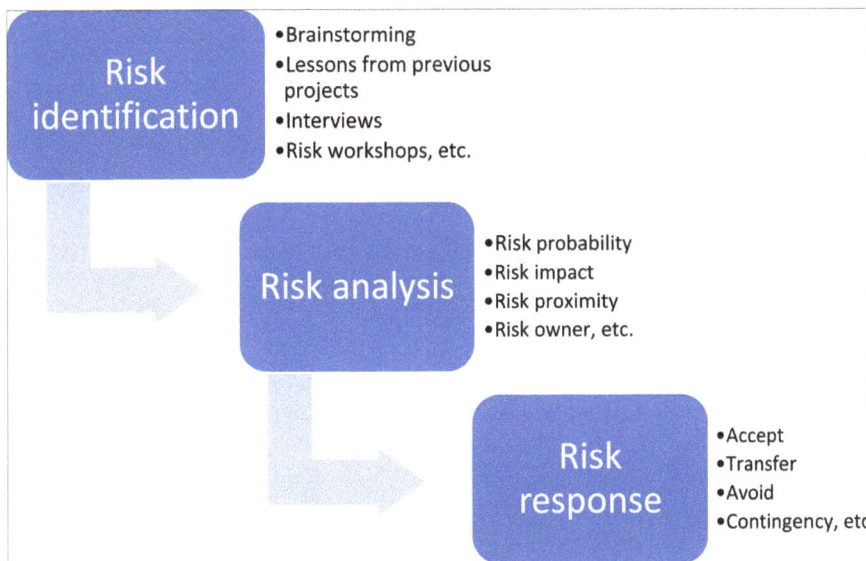

Figure 19.3 Risk management steps

Summary

Having read this chapter you should now be aware of and able to:

– Define the term 'risk'
– Explain the purpose of risk management
– Outline the stages of a typical risk management process (including identification, analysis, response and closure)
– Describe the use of risk registers

End-of-chapter assessment – dealing with risks

Exercise 1 – The humanitarian mission project

a. Using the case study topic of the humanitarian mission project list some of the risks you can think of

b. Use the risks identified to prepare a risk register for the project (focus only on the top 10 risks)

Exercise 2 – The humanitarian mission project

1   **Risk can be defined as:**

   A. An uncertain event or set of circumstances that, should it/they occur, will influence the achievement of one or more objectives

   B. Anything that can happen on a project and affect it negatively

   C. Anything the project manager has no control over

   D. Uncertain events that can cost money and impact on health and safety

2   **Risk management allows individual risk events and overall risks to be:**

   A. Understood and proactively managed to minimise threats and maximise opportunities

   B. Proactively managed to remove threats and maximise opportunities

   C. Managed in a way that will minimise threats and maximise opportunities

   D. Found and transferred to another organisation

3   **Risk management:**

   A. Ensures risks are proactively managed

   B. Helps to foresee what could possibly affect the project either positively or negatively

   C. Is an intentional approach to minimise threats and maximise opportunities

   D. All of the above

4   **The risk management process follows this sequence:**

A. Initiate, Identify, Assess, Respond, Implement

B. Identify, Initiate, Assess, Implement, Respond

C. Initiate, Assess, Respond, Identify, Implement

D. Identify, Respond, Initiate, Assess, Respond

5   **Which one of these is not a function of the risk register?**

A. Records identified risks

B. Records responses to risks

C. Records the risk impact and likelihood

D. Records issues

6   **Which one of the following is not an appropriate risk response?**

A. Avoid

B. Transfer

C. Accept

D. Expand

CHAPTER 20

DEALING WITH ISSUES

By the end of this chapter you should be able to:

- Define the term 'issue'
- Outline the purpose of issue management
- Differentiate between an issue and a risk
- State the stages of an issue resolution process

20.1 Project issues

> **An Issue** is a problem that has happened on the project for which the project manager is unable to deal with by themselves. Project issues should usually be escalated for resolution.

An issue occurs when a situation on the project is beyond the project manager's delegated authority to resolve by themselves. Usually, when issues arise on projects, the project manager will be required to escalate this from one management level to the next for resolution.

An issue is anything that has occurred on the project that the project manager cannot resolve by themselves.

In project management, situations and problems sometimes arise. Some of these the project manager can resolve, others they may not be able to resolve by themselves and will require a superior decision. When such a problem requires more than just the project manager in order for it to be resolved, that problem or situation will be called an ISSUE.

Issues, just like changes, should be recorded on a register called the **ISSUES LOG**. This register should be reviewed regularly by the relevant parties and decision(s) to deal with them made.

The process by which the concerns that threaten the project objectives and which cannot be resolved by the project manager are **identified, escalated** and **addressed** is called **issue management.**

During project delivery, issues will be actively recorded as they arise and appropriately escalated for resolution.

An example of an issue may be a key member of the team deciding to resign.

20.2 Differences between issues and risks

Table 20.1 Differences between risk and issue

Risk	Issue
Think of risk as events or conditions that might happen in the future. Example: a critical resource might leave the project.	Something that has happened and needs to be resolved by another, superior to the project manager.
Project team members might be injured by the new equipment.	A team member is seriously injured by the new equipment.

Risk	Issue
The project manager deals with the risk.	The project sponsor deals with the issue.
There may be unanticipated requirement changes.	A new requirement has been agreed and needs to be incorporated into the project.
Protestors might be angered during the project delivery and decide to demonstrate.	Protestors have started demonstrations on the project site.
Sometimes, when a risk materialises, it becomes an issue.	

20.3 Issue resolution process

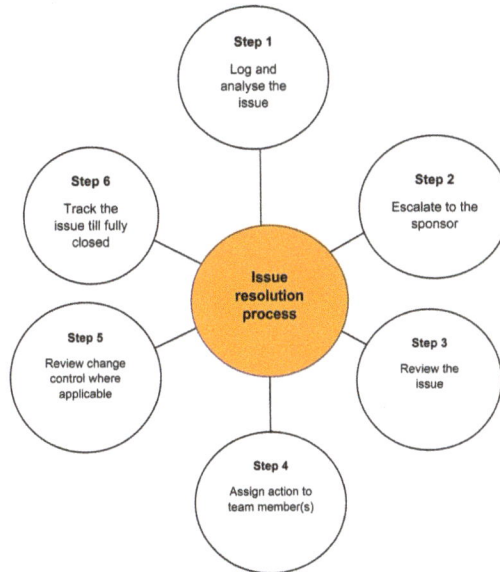

Figure 20.1 Issue resolution steps

Summary

Having read this chapter you should now be aware of and able to:

– Define the term 'issue'
– Outline the purpose of issue management
– Differentiate between an issue and a risk
– State the stages of an issue resolution process

End-of-chapter test – dealing with issues

Exercise 1 – The humanitarian mission project

1   An issue can be defined as:

A. Anything the project manager cannot deal with as soon as possible

B. When the tolerance of delegated work is predicted to be exceeded or has exceeded

C. A threat to the project objectives which cannot be resolved by the project sponsor

D. Any situation which arises when the project implementation starts

2   When an issue occurs, the project manager is expected to:

A. Escalate the issue from one level of management to the other for resolution

B. Try and resolve this to the best of their ability

C. Ignore it and hope it goes away

D. Record the issue and move on to complete the project quickly

3   You are managing a project when a critical team member suddenly resigns. This is:

A. An issue

B. A risk

C. Both a risk and an issue

D. All of the above

4   Issues are recorded in:

A. The project management plan

B. The project risk register

C. The project log book

D. The issues log

CHAPTER 21

UNDERSTANDING COMMUNICATION

By the end of this chapter you should be able to:

- Define the term 'communication'
- Outline the advantages of different communication methods (including face-to-face, physical and virtual)
- Outline the disadvantages of different communication methods (including face-to-face, physical and virtual)
- Outline the content of a communication plan
- Explain the benefits, to a project manager, of a communication plan

21.1 Understanding communication

> **Communication** is the process or an act of transferring information and ensuring that there is a common understanding. Communication can be written, verbal, non-verbal or virtual.

Communication can be broken down as the giving, receiving, processing and interpreting of information. Communication can be conveyed verbally, non-verbally, actively, passively, formally, informally, consciously or unconsciously.

21.1.2 Key points about communication

- Communication during project delivery is essential to the successful delivery of that project.
- Communication should be clear and well delivered if you want to avoid misunderstanding with project information, requirements, instructions, etc.
- It will be essential for the project manager to communicate effectively with the stakeholders, project sponsor, project team and all other relevant organisations involved in the successful implementation of the project.
- During communication, the sender transmits information using an **appropriate communication medium** which the intended recipient should be able to receive and understand in the way it is intended to be understood.
- As the project manager, you must choose and use appropriate communication methods for communicating project information.
- Communication can easily be misunderstood or misinterpreted depending on many factors, such as: **appearance, expression, posture, tone, pitch, pace, volume**, etc.

Examples of communication methods/mediums

Table 21.1 Communication methods

Email	Telephone	Reports	Catch-up meeting
Formal meeting	Face-to-face conversation	Social media	SMS

Whilst any of the above methods can be used, it is fundamental that the appropriate medium is always used to communicate information.

21.2 Advantages and disadvantages of different communication methods

Table 21.2 Advantages and disadvantages of verbal communication

Verbal communication	
Listening/talking to a person verbally	
Advantages	**Disadvantages**
– Quick and easy – Cheaper – Saves time – Persuasion can be used immediately – Clarification can be offered immediately	– Accent may cause differences in understanding – Speed of speech can make it difficult to understand – Cultural differences may affect understanding – There may not be the chance to hear again – Prone to different interpretation – Cannot be relied upon as evidence in a court of law – No record available unless recorded – Legally not valid

Table 21.3 Advantages and disadvantages of non - verbal communication

Non-verbal communication	
Communicating through body language, signs, gestures, etc.	
Advantages	**Disadvantages**
– Can reinforce verbal communication – Provides clues – Can send a strong positive message (dressing, posture, etc.) – Can be used to express emotions/feelings better and more easily (e.g. emojis)	– May be perceived wrongly (depending on culture) – May not be easy to understand – Can contradict what is being said verbally, making interpretation difficult – Can send the wrong or negative impression

Table 21.4 Advantages and disadvantages of written communication

Written communication	
Communicating through reading/writing	
Advantages	**Disadvantages**
– Easy to understand – Can be used as evidence – Is very reliable and effective – Can be reread several times for understanding	– Non-verbal cues absent so interpretation could be difficult – May be difficult to articulate views – Takes longer – Not effective when instant views and opinions are needed

Table 21.5 Advantages and disadvantages of virtual communication

Virtual communication	
Communicating through virtual means: Skype, conference call, video, etc.	
Advantages	**Disadvantages**
– Convenient – Cheaper: saves travel time and meeting rooms, etc. – Can offer flexibility to participants – Helps with productivity and efficiency – Ideal when a physical meeting is impossible	– People can easily be distracted and do unrelated stuff – Connection may be broken – Can have issues with technology – Poor connection (internet) can affect communication

Table 21.6 Advantages and disadvantages of face to face communication

Face-to-face	
Communicating face-to-face with someone	
Advantages	**Disadvantages**
– Quick/saves time – Can obtain instant feedback – Can tell if the listener is paying attention/focusing	– Cultural difference – Fluency of language – Language barrier – You may not be able to hide emotions

Table 21.7 Advantages and disadvantages of visual communication

Visual	
Communicating through images, pictures, drawings, art, charts, graphs, etc.	
Advantages	**Disadvantages**
– Can send a message that may require many words to explain – Can be used to express feelings or convey emotions better – Can be catchy – Can be easily understood – Can be understood irrespective of language	– May sometimes require words to explain – Can be misinterpreted – May be difficult to understand

21.3 Factors that impact the effectiveness of communication

☐ Cultural background
☐ Mood
☐ Current environment
☐ Team dynamics
☐ Team location
☐ Working environment
☐ Lack of common language or understanding across disciplines
☐ Attitudes, emotions, prejudices
☐ Assumptions about the sender/receiver
☐ Noise, surroundings
☐ Withholding information
☐ Ambiguous messages

21.4 How to enhance the effectiveness of communication

☐ Simplify the message
☐ Obtain feedback and work on using it to improve future communications
☐ Follow a standard where applicable
☐ Use an agreed format where applicable
☐ Target audience and medium to the message and make it relevant

☐ Prepare and use a project communication plan to aid effective communication
☐ Develop effective listening skills
☐ Use reinforcement with actions
☐ Be mindful of sensitivities and adopt a communication style

21.5 Communication plan

✓ Typically, the project communication plan identifies the information to be communicated; to whom, when, why, how, which medium, etc.
✓ As part of the **communication plan**, you will develop a strategy for sharing and maintaining stakeholder engagement throughout the project.
✓ Prior to communicating, it is advisable to learn more about your stakeholders and their organisations: key contacts, personnel changes, communication channels and feedback methods, etc. This helps you to be up to date with your communication and engagement.
✓ The communication plan should identify **who** the stakeholders are, **why** you need to communicate with them, **what** you intend to communicate, **how often** and the **method** you intend to use. Where applicable, decide or determine a method you will use to measure how effective the communication/engagement is.

21.5.1 A typical communication plan will capture:

☐ What should be communicated
☐ Who should receive this message
☐ Who will communicate this message
☐ Why they should receive this message
☐ When the communication should be sent
☐ How they should receive the communication (appropriate medium)
☐ Frequency of communication

Table 21.8 The project communication plan example

What to communicate	Who should receive	Who should send	Why they are receiving	When they should receive	Medium	Frequency
Monthly report	Chief executive	Project sponsor	Keep informed	Monthly	Email report	Once a month
Meeting minutes	All stakeholders	Project manager	Keep informed	After meetings	Email minutes	As required

21.6 Benefits of an effective communication plan

Table 21.9 Benefits of effective communication plan

Efficiency	The right amount and targeted information is sent as per the communication plan.
Information	The project team always has the relevant information readily available to share, making it more efficient. The team doesn't waste time trying to find the information it needs.
Quality	Proper communication can be linked to quality project delivery as this ensures the right and relevant information without ambiguity is communicated at all times.
Risk avoidance	Good communication minimises the likelihood of errors and potential mistakes. In doing so, potential project risks are avoided.
Stakeholder support	Effective and good communication planning ensures stakeholder support for the project is generated and maintained.
Clear communication	The project team can communicate clearly and effectively and thereby avoid potentially costly mistakes.

Summary

Having read this chapter you should now be aware of and able to:

- Define the term 'communication'
- Outline the advantages of different communication methods (including face-to-face, physical and virtual)
- Outline the disadvantages of different communication methods (including face-to-face, physical and virtual)
- Outline the content of a communication plan
- Explain the benefits, to a project manager, of a communication plan

End-of-chapter assessment – communication

Exercise 1 – The humanitarian mission project

Using the case study topic of the humanitarian mission project, prepare a communication plan for the stakeholders identified for this project.

Exercise 2 – The humanitarian mission project

1   Communication can be defined as:

A. The means by which social media, email, text, etc. is used to transmit project information

B. The means by which information or instructions are exchanged

C. The method by which we transmit information from one point to another

D. The means by which project stakeholder information is properly communicated by the project manager

2   Communication is successful only when:

A. The received meaning is the same as the transmitted meaning

B. The person on the receiving end is comfortable and happy with the message

C. The information communicated is not offensive

D. All of the above

3   Which of these is the least preferred communication method in project delivery:

A. Email

B. Letter

C. Phone call

D. WhatsApp

4   You have been asked to send a project update to the project sponsor; which of these may not be an appropriate communication medium to use?

A. Email

B. Face-to-face

C. Report

D. Text

5   Cultural background, working environment, noise, surroundings and location can all be classed as:

A. Barriers to effective communication

B. Strategies for effective communication

C. Ideas the project manager can use to promote effective communication

D. All of the above

6   You have met a visitor from another country who appears to be stranded and confused. Their understanding of the local language is very limited, so you are finding it difficult to communicate. Which one of these approaches will make the communication worse?

A. Simplifying your message

B. Obtaining feedback to check understanding

C. Developing effective listening skills

D. Pretending to understand what they are saying

7   To facilitate good communication, you must not:

A. Use reinforcement with actions

B. Be mindful of sensitivities and adapt your communication style

C. Target the audience and medium to the message and make it relevant

D. Only communicate in writing for record keeping

8   The plan which identifies what information is to be communicated, to whom, why, when, where, how, through which medium and the desired impact, is called the:

A. Communication monitoring plan

B. Communication plan

C. Stakeholder communication plan

D. Engagement plan

9   It is beneficial to develop a plan for communicating with your stakeholders. Which one of these is not a benefit for developing this plan?

A. Promotes efficiency

B. Makes information available

C. Promotes quality

D. Promotes the project manager and the sponsor

CHAPTER 22

UNDERSTANDING LEADERSHIP

By the end of this chapter you should be able to:

- Define the term 'leadership'
- Outline some leadership strategies
- Outline some leadership styles

22.1 Understanding leadership

> **Leadership** is the ability of an individual, an organisation, group, or team to be able to establish a vision influence and guide other individuals, teams, organisations towards that vision.

Project leaders support the team members to follow the right path, do what is expected and/or do the right things.

As a leader you will set direction, build an inspiring vision, and influence and align the members to follow that vision. Leadership is about having a strategy that will help the team to perform.

A good leader will always provide a clear vision, direction, inspiration and support to the followers. In contrast, there are also less experienced leaders who behave in ways that unknowingly impact negatively on their followers and the team.

Projects involve bringing people together as a team to achieve a specific project deliverable, and therefore the project manager as the leader of the project team must exhibit the right leadership skills to motivate the team to work together towards a common vision.

22.2 Leadership strategies

As a project manager, you are also seen as a leader managing a team and must be fully aware of some of the key leadership strategies.
- You must be aware that the project team may not usually be your direct report within the organisational structure. Team members may have their lines of reporting as part of their day to day roles.
- In effect, the team's willingness, and ability to follow the project manager could be affected by things like their priorities, loyalty, and demands placed on them by their direct managers, etc.
- Be aware as a project manager and leader that the team members may need to be motivated differently if you want to get the best out of them
- You may sometimes be expected to coach, and mentor project team members as required to enhance growth and development, especially for junior members of the team
- As the project leader, dealing with stakeholders and leading them can sometimes present some challenges, a great level of care and approach is always required often

the need to adapt your leadership approach to suit the situation will be fundamental. This is called **situational leadership**

– You must be aware of the fundamental leadership approaches and apply them accordingly if you are to lead a successful project team.

22.3 Understanding leadership

When individuals with varying skills, abilities and personalities come together to work towards a specific project vision, it will take a good leader to be able to hold them together and provide the vision, direction and inspiration in order for the team to perform.

The individual project team members may have great abilities, talents and skills; however, to work and complement each other with their varying skills, personalities and habits, they will require a leader who fully understands how to set the vision, provide direction and inspire the team towards a common goal.

As a project leader, you will not only be giving instructions, your role goes beyond that and takes into consideration some of the core leadership traits as shown in the table below.

22.4 The project manager as a leader

Table 22.1 The project manager as a leader

The project manager as a leader
Maintains and promotes the project vision
Creates a good environment for the team to perform
Adapts and varies their leadership style to suit the team members
Resolves conflict and provides constructive feedback
Focuses on developing the individuals in the team
Sets clear SMART objectives for the team
Always communicates effectively with the team
Ensures relevant project details are properly communicated to the team
Ensures the team works together by showing good leadership. The project manager should also keep team members motivated.
Supports individuals in their personal and career development aspirations

22.5 Examples of leadership styles

Authoritarian leadership (autocratic)	•Leader makes independent decisions •Followers must obey the leader •Followers feel controlled •Only good when little or no time to debate
Participative leadership (democratic)	•Leader makes decisions by consulting followers •Followers are guided rather than instructed •Followers able to express their views •Leader makes final decision after considering views •Followers feel more important and show more commitment
Delegative leadership (laissez-faire)	•Leader gives little or no guidance •Followers tend to make their own decisions •Not good for inexperienced followers
Transformational leadership	•Inspires and motivates followers towards a common vision •Leader develops the followers •Followers tend to be satisfied
Situational leadership	•Leadership style changes to suit the situation •Leader adopts different leadership positions: telling, selling, participating and delegating •A combination of all the leadership styles above
Transactional leadership	•The leader-follower relationship is more of a transaction •Followers agree to follow a set of instructions and are punished for non-compliance

Figure 22.1 Leadership styles

Summary

Having read this chapter you should now be aware of and able to:

– Define the term 'leadership'
– Outline some leadership strategies
– Outline some leadership styles

End-of-chapter assessment – leadership

Exercise 1 – The humanitarian mission project

1   **Leadership can be defined as:**

    A. The ability to force people to follow your instructions

    B. The ability to establish vision and direction to convince and lead others towards your personal goals

    C. The ability to establish vision and direction, to influence and align others towards a common purpose and to empower and inspire people to achieve project success

    D. The process of establishing vision and direction, to influence and align others towards a common goal and force them to achieve project success

2   **Which of these is not a characteristic of an authoritative leader?**

    A. Makes independent decisions

    B. Usually controls the followers

    C. Expects the followers to obey without disputing

    D. Is intellectual and well educated

3   **Which one is not a characteristic of a good leader?**

    A. Is aware of the team's motivational requirements

    B. Provides constructive and immediate feedback

    C. Embraces feedback from the team on their own performance

    D. Forms a team of intelligent members

4   **A leadership style that changes with the situation is:**

    A. Flexible leadership

    B. Situational leadership

    C. Delegative leadership

    D. Participative leadership

5   **A leader who often gives little or no guidance and tends to allow followers to make their own decisions will most likely be:**

A. An authoritarian leader

B. A delegative leader

C. A transformational leader

D. A situational leader

CHAPTER 23

UNDERSTANDING TEAMWORK

By the end of this chapter you should be able to:

– Explain how a project team leader can influence team performance

– Outline the challenges to a project manager when developing and leading a project team

– Outline how a project manager can use models to assist team development (including Belbin and Tuckman)

23.1 Project team

A project team can be described as a set of individuals, groups and/or organisations responsible to the project manager for working towards a common purpose.

> **A Team** is a group of individuals working collaboratively towards achieving a common goal.

A team can be described as a group of individuals who are working together collaboratively towards a common purpose. Team members usually come with complementary skills that make the team perform better together than individuals who make up the team.

A team will usually have shared goals with a common approach to doing things. They hold each other accountable if they are to perform effectively.

Effective team performance is **not** only based on the technical abilities or intelligence of the team members but also on other aspects of individual abilities, such as their **ability to solve problems, make decisions, plan, find information, check facts, etc.** A team with such a variety of individuals performs much more effectively.

Naturally, people are different, with varying strengths, weaknesses, habits and personalities. These attributes in people make individuals **unique**. It also means that when people come together to work on a project, they will come with these skills and personalities.

A good team is not built on individuals who share the same strengths and characteristics but on individuals with varying attributes, skills and personalities. When a team includes individuals who are good at different roles, that team is far more likely to be effective and successful.

Team members are meant to work to complement each other towards a common vision. What one individual cannot achieve on their own may be achievable within a team.

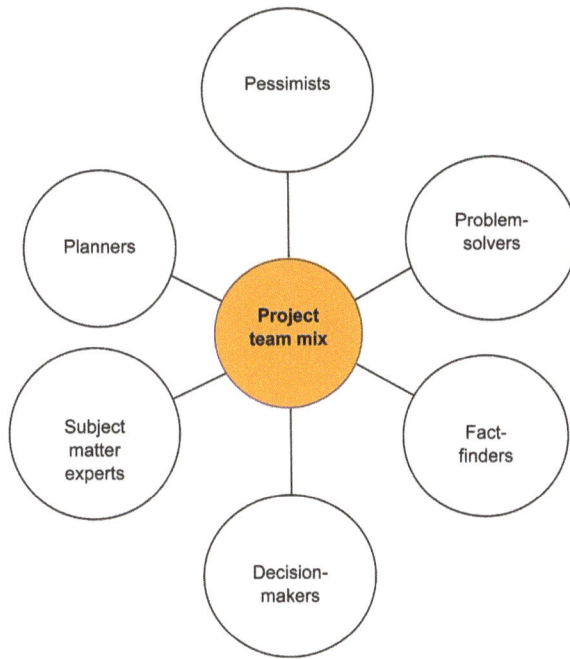

Figure 23.1 The project team matrix

23.2 Team performance

According to **Bruce Tuckman**, who first developed this model, he found that when individuals first come together to form a team, they develop through certain dynamics before beginning to perform as a team.

He concluded that a typical team develops through stages of: FORMING, STORMING, NORMING, PERFORMING and ADJOURNING.

Table 23.1 Bruce Tuckman team performance stages

Stage	Description/Characteristics
Forming	– New project team forms – Individuals are given the project objectives – There is confusion at the initial stage – Some team members may be testing the boundaries – Others may not be sure of each other or team members – Team members try to figure out how to work with each other – **As a leader,** you must ensure the project objectives are very clear at this stage

Stage	Description/Characteristics
Storming	– Team members begin to work on the project – Often, conflict about status arises – Members compete to get their ideas accepted – Differences in opinions become visible – There are lots of conflicts at this stage – **As a leader**, you must support and assist the team to work collaboratively – You must establish guidelines for team working – Beware that team members may struggle to move past this stage if not well managed
Norming	– Team members begin to accept each other and work together – A good team spirit begins to develop – Team members begin to trust each other – The team members at this stage are seeking each other out and assisting one another – The team makes key decisions amongst themselves – There is real progress with the work
Performing	– This is a highly performing team – They are seeking to reach a collective goal – They win as a team and fail as a team – The team is so highly effective that they do not need the leader to instruct them daily; they know what to do – The team communicates openly and honestly – The team is now able to accomplish great work
Adjourning	– The project is now complete, and the team must be dissolved – It is possible that team members may feel anxious and sad about the dissolution

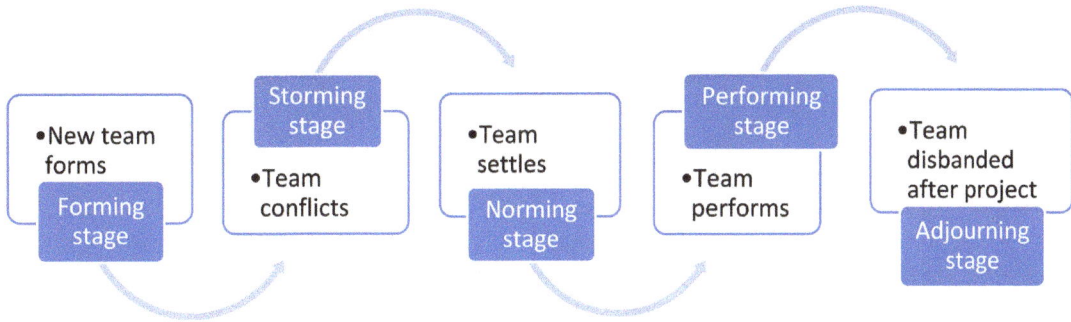

Figure 23.2 Team performance stages

23.3 Barriers to effective teamwork

Table 23.2 Barriers to effective teamwork

Barriers to effective teamwork
Lack of or poor communication strategy; team members do not understand what is communicated and do not know what is going on
Lack of a common brief or understanding of the do's and don'ts of the team
Individuals performing roles that do not play to their strengths
Lack of direction and motivation
Lack of or poor leadership
Personality clashes within the team
Discrimination within the team

23.4 Team models

Managers should consider several factors when developing a team and be aware that individuals have **different skills** and **personalities.**

Team members may come from different cultures and working environments, which can affect team performance.

The establishment of a team will initially involve the selection of individuals based on their **skills, behaviours** and **attitudes.** Team-working therefore becomes most effective when people with **complementary** skills and behaviours are committed to a common objective and method of working.

Belbin and Margerison-McCann's team model is an excellent way to illustrate how different individuals with different personalities can work together as an effective team.

These models have established that every individual comes packaged with unique strengths, weaknesses, forming the basis of our personalities. Within the team, one person's strengths will balance another's weaknesses, making individuals perform better in a team context than as individuals, especially if team members are given roles that play to their strengths. According to Bruce Tuckman, when teams first come together, they will not start as high performing from the start. That team develops through a series of developmental stages, according to Bruce Tuckman.

Generally, people tend to be better at doing the things they enjoy. As a manager, you need to understand everyone's preferences to help bring together a group of people who have the 'right' strengths and abilities to support the project. It can be established from the models that every individual comes packaged with unique strengths and weaknesses. These are usually manifested in a team setting where our strengths will balance another's weaknesses.

23.5 Margerison-McCann Team Management Profile

Team management is another profile developed by Dr. Charles Margerison and Dr. Dick McCann. Their team management profile is based on a person's role preferences. In all, they identified eight role preferences under four broad team performance areas – **advisers, explorers, organisers, and controllers** – to support the development of the team management preference shown below.

The Margerison-McCann team preference

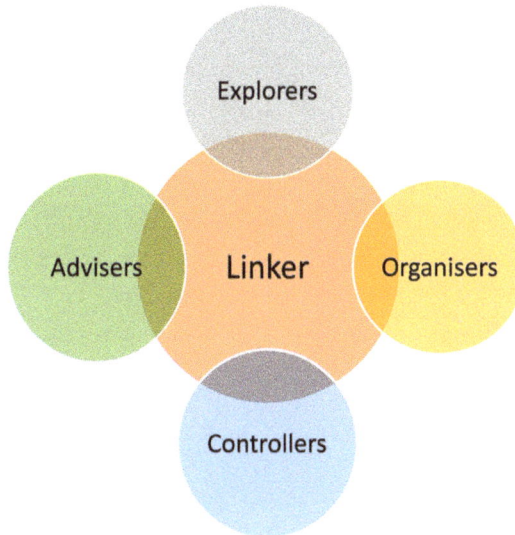

Figure 23.3 The Margerison-McCann team preference

The role preferences are as follows:

Table 23.3 The Margerison-McCann team roles

Reporter-Adviser	Enjoys giving and gathering information
Creator-Innovator	Likes to come up with new ideas and different approaches to tasks
Explorer-Promoter	Enjoys exploring possibilities and looking for new opportunities
Assessor-Developer	Prefers analysing new opportunities and making them work in practice
Thruster-Organiser	Likes to push forward and get results
Concluder-Producer	Prefers to work in a systematic way to produce work outputs
Controller-Inspector	Enjoys focusing on the detailed and controlling aspects of work
Upholder-Maintainer	Likes to uphold standards and values and maintain team excellence
The 'Linker' role, shown in the centre of the wheel, involves integrating and coordinating the work of others within the team and in relation to external interfaces. This role has to be performed by everyone, although the team leader has a particular responsibility here.	

These roles are quite like Belbin's model, although they are not identical. It tends to imply that a person will usually lean towards and enjoy certain roles. In a team setting, there are likely to be individuals exhibiting different attributes, which brings variety and strength to the team. For example, the Margerison-McCann model assumes that people are more motivated to perform the 'types of work' they prefer.

Their profile report helps managers to understand why people are motivated to perform some roles and not others. The Margerison-McCann model displays some similarities with Belbin's model. They both conclude that specific individuals will prefer certain types of functions. Margerison-McCann concludes that certain people are more motivated when given tasks or types of work that they like.

Their profile report provides a good insight into an individual's motivational needs. Managers can understand and benefit from knowing how team members are motivated to do some work types and not others.

23.6 Belbin team roles

This team model was originally developed by Dr. Meredith Belbin in 1969 as a cluster of nine behaviours called '**team roles**'.

The conclusion from his work was that team members have both strengths and weaknesses that they bring into a team. Some teams may have access to all the nine roles others may have less. Regardless, it needs team members with a mixture of the roles for a team to perform at its best.

As a leader, you must be aware that you do not need each of the nine team roles at the same time for a team to perform.

Table 23.4 The nine Belbin roles

The nine Belbin roles	
Coordinator	Able to get others working to a shared aim – confident/mature
Resource investigator	Uses their inquisitive nature to find ideas to bring back to the team – outgoing and enthusiastic but can forget to follow up
Team worker	Helps the team to gel, using their versatility to identify the work required and complete it on behalf of the team
Plant	Tends to be highly creative and good at solving problems in unconventional ways

The nine Belbin roles	
Monitor evaluator	Provides a logical eye, making impartial judgements where required, and weighs up the team's options in a dispassionate way
Specialist	Brings in-depth knowledge of a key area to the team – single-minded, self-starting and dedicated
Shaper	Provides the necessary drive to ensure that the team keeps moving and does not lose focus or momentum
Implementer	Needed to plan a workable strategy and carry it out as efficiently as possible
Completer/finisher	Most effectively used at the end of tasks to polish and scrutinise the work for errors, subjecting it to the highest standards of quality control

Summary

Having read this chapter you should now be aware of and able to:

– Explain how a project team leader can influence team performance
– Outline the challenges to a project manager when developing and leading a project team
– Outline how a project manager can use models to assist team development (including Belbin and Tuckman)

End-of-chapter assessment – understanding teamwork

Exercise 1 – The humanitarian mission project

1 Which of the following will not help the project manager to influence team performance?

A. Creating a good environment for the team to perform

B. Adapting and varying leadership style to suit team members

C. Setting clear SMART objectives for the team

D. Leaving the responsibility of the team cohesion to the team members

2 A manager who supports their team members in their personal and career development aspirations will:

A. Be able to influence team performance by that support

B. Be able to minimise family tensions in the team member's family

C. Allow the team members to respect the manager

D. Minimise project risk and issues

3 Which one of these is not a characteristic of a project team?

A. A group of people with complementary skills committed to a common purpose

B. A group of people working collaboratively together

C. A group of people with shared goals

D. A group of people with similar skills committed to a common purpose

4 When a group first comes together to form a team, according to Bruce Tuckman the group will go through these dynamics:

A. Forming, Storming, Norming, Performing, Adjourning

B. Storming, Forming, Norming, Performing, Adjourning

C. Norming, Forming, Performing, Adjourning, Storming

D. Adjourning, Storming, Forming, Performing, Norming

5   **Which one is not a barrier to effective teamwork?**

A. Lack of direction and motivation

B. Personality clashes within the team

C. Discrimination within the team

D. Individuals performing roles that play to their strengths

6   **Which of these can be attributed to the Margerison-McCann team model?**

A. Most people do not enjoy their work

B. There are nine personality types

C. Individuals will perform better in a team context if they are given roles that play to their strengths

D. There are eight role preferences

7   **Dr Meredith Belbin's team model indicates that our behaviours can be grouped into nine clusters. Which one is an incorrect explanation?**

A. Coordinators – able to get others working on a shared aim

B. Team workers – help the team to gel

C. Plant – environmental activist in the team

D. Monitor – provides a logical eye, making impartial judgements

8   **According to Bruce Tuckman, when are team members likely to feel settled and comfortable with their roles?**

A. Norming stage

B. Forming stage

C. Adjourning stage

D. Storming stage

CHAPTER 24

PROJECTS AND THE REGULATORY FRAMEWORK

By the end of this chapter you should be able to:

- Outline why the project manager may have to understand the legal framework when managing projects

- State some of the main legal frameworks a project may have to abide by

24.1 Regulatory framework

> All projects are delivered within a geographic location
> which often has legal and regulatory frameworks specific
> to that location or the industry within which
> the project is carried out

Project work does not happen in a vacuum; its delivery is always affected and somewhat dictated by the relevant regulatory and legal frameworks pertaining to the geographic area within which it is carried out. For example, delivering a project in an airport environment may require adhering to specific regulations, acts, laws, etc. that pertain to the aviation industry, e.g. aviation security compliance, emissions, noise, etc. Likewise, two similar projects may be governed differently in two different countries because of the regulatory framework that governs projects in those countries.

24.2 The project professional and the regulatory framework

As a project professional, it is your responsibility to be aware of and keep up to date with existing, new, and changes in, regulations, laws, directives, etc. that may affect your project.

Depending on the geographic location, the organisation or industry, specific regulations may also apply.

For example, delivering a project that involves asbestos in the UK will require very strict rules regarding safeguarding the health, safety and welfare of anyone that may be affected. There are specific regulations which make it mandatory to carry out certain duties when dealing with asbestos, for example, controlling exposure to asbestos.

Conversely, asbestos control may not be banned or highly regulated in other geographic locations, which may imply that the project professional may not be required by law to follow specific processes in managing or dealing with asbestos.

It is the responsibility of the project professional to engage or employ the services of known experts in the specific aspects of the project that require compliance with the law. For example, in the UK, construction activities are dealt with and managed under the **Construction (Design and Management) Regulations (CDM Regulations or CDM)**. The regulations set out clearly what to do to secure the health and safety of anyone who may be affected by the work. There are other regulations and acts that govern different types of projects.

It will be the responsibility of the project professional to follow and apply all required guidance and procedures as set out in law that are applicable to the project's geographic location.

It is not enough to say you did not know. In a court of law, being ignorant about the law, regulation, Act of Parliament, etc. is not an excuse to break it or avoid prosecution.

24.3 Health and safety

Within an organisation, it is the duty of management to ensure that projects under their control comply with the relevant health and safety legislation.

As the project professional, you may not be expected to know of every applicable law, regulation, guidance, etc. and be an expert in them; however, it is your **responsibility** to seek **competent advice** to assist you to discharge your duties and responsibilities.

Health and safety requirements and legislation may vary from country to country. In the UK, for example, the two key pieces of notable legislation governing health, safety and welfare are:

o   **Health and Safety at Work Act 1974**
o   **Management of Health and Safety at Work Regulations 1999**

The **Health and Safety at Work Act** places a requirement on employers to secure the health, safety and welfare of their employees and to ensure that those who may be affected by the works are protected.

The **Management of Health and Safety at Work Regulations,** on the other hand, require for risk assessments to be undertaken and for competent advice to be sought.

24.4 Implications of non-compliance

Usually there are consequences for not complying with specific laws, regulations, directives, Acts of Parliament, etc.

These are not there to make project work difficult, neither are they there to trip up the project professional or test their level of intelligence. They are instituted for very good reasons: some to protect and secure the health, safety and welfare of all the people who may be affected, some to help economies to function well. They may be there to protect the rights of individuals and bring about uniformity, etc.

Non-conformance may therefore carry sanctions, warnings, fines, etc. The severity of the sanction or fine will depend on the impact or the likely impact of the non-compliance.

Summary

Having read this chapter you should now be aware of and able to:

– Outline why the project manager may have to understand the legal framework when managing projects
– State some of the main legal frameworks a project may have to abide by

End-of-chapter assessment – projects and the regulatory framework

Exercise 1 – The humanitarian mission project

> Using the case study topic of the humanitarian mission project, list some of the regulations, laws, acts, etc. that the project may be required to abide by.

Exercise 2 – The humanitarian mission project

1   As the project professional, you:
   A. Must be familiar with all the regulations that impact on your project
   B. Must be able to read and interpret what the law requires on your project
   C. Do not need to be an expert in any of the regulations as long as you can seek competent advice and guidance
   D. Only need to be an expert in health and safety regulations

2   Which of these is not the main reason for ensuring projects abide by the relevant laws and regulations:
   A. To protect and secure the health, safety and welfare of everyone
   B. To help the economy
   C. To protect the right of individuals, teams, organisations, etc.
   D. To make project delivery look professional

3   Health and safety management is the process of:
   A. Reducing accidents and injury to workmen
   B. Identifying threats to workers
   C. Identifying and minimising threats to workers and to those affected by the work during the deployment stage
   D. Identifying and minimising threats to workers and to those affected by the work throughout the project life cycle

4   **The two principal health and safety legislations in the UK are:**

A. Health and Safety at Work Act 1973 and Management of Health and Safety at Work Regulations 1999

B. Health and Safety at Work Act 1963 and Management of Health and Safety at Work Regulations 1998

C. Health and Safety at Work Act 1974 and Management of Health and Safety at Work Regulations 1999

D. Health and Safety at Work Act 1999 and Management of Health and Safety at Work Regulations 1974

5   **Project professionals are required to know all the regulations pertaining to their projects within a given geographic location:**

A. True

B. False

CHAPTER 25

PROJECT REVIEWS

By the end of this chapter you should be able to:

- Explain the purpose of project reviews
- Explain the benefits of different types of reviews: gate reviews, audits, post-project reviews and benefit reviews

25.1 Project reviews

Project reviews help to provide insight into what is happening within our projects. As a health check-up is to a person, so is a review of a project. Reviews provide an independent perspective of what is happening on the project. They are critical in project management, ensuring better project performance because:

– They offer an independent view of the project status
– They give an insight into how the project is performing against expectations
– The project review results help the project manager identify and understand missing knowledge and gaps with their project management approach.

Reviews are also beneficial to the project sponsor and management because:

– They provide a clear and better insight into the project performance.
– They allow management to make better decisions about the project; whether to cancel, suspend, redirect resources, change direction, or continue.
– They help to ensure that critical decisions are based on facts and data rather than assumptions and feelings.
– It helps organisations and teams to learn from experience, mistakes, good practice, etc.
– They promote the use of project lessons learned culture.
– A good understanding of what is happening on our projects makes it easier to make the right decisions on projects.
– Reviews provide clear and well-validated information to decision-makers.

Figure 25.1 Types of project reviews

25.2 Purpose of different types of reviews

Table 25.1 Purpose of different types of project reviews

Gate reviews/ Decision gates	The progression from one life cycle stage to another is also a time to **review** and assess the project prior to deciding to progress to the next stage. This passage of the project from one cycle stage to the next is termed 'the gateway', hence the term gate review/ decision gate. This is the review that happens in between project phases/stages. The gate review allows senior management or the project sponsor to decide to continue the project or not based on the review findings.
Post-project reviews	This is another type of review undertaken only after the project has been completed and handed over but before the project is finally closed out. The post-project review is nearly the same as capturing and recording project lessons. This review allows the project team to learn lessons while they are still fresh and record and document them for the benefit of future projects.
Benefits reviews	This is also another review carried out to identify whether the intended project benefits have been realised or are being realised. Benefit realisation is the accountability of the project sponsor. Every project is undertaken to deliver benefits, which makes this review important because it helps to confirm whether the intended benefits have been realised.
Peer reviews	This type of review is the same as asking a colleague or a peer to check your work for you. It is informal but can be a very powerful tool for pointing out errors and omissions or even sharing ideas and experiences on projects.
Project audits	This is a more formal review carried out by an external party to the project. It can be carried out by the project office. The purpose is to ensure the project aligns with the expected processes and that they are being delivered as planned. Following an audit, a report is usually produced which identifies any areas of weakness, non-compliance, etc. that must be addressed.

End-of-chapter assessment – reviews

Exercise 1 – The humanitarian mission project

Using the humanitarian mission project, you have been appointed as the independent person responsible for ensuring the project follows the appropriate processes and is delivered in accordance with the agreed processes. What type of review(s) will you use and what will you want to get out of it?

Exercise 2 – The humanitarian mission project

1   **Which one of these is not a good reason for carrying out project reviews?**

   A. To give an insight into what is happening on the project

   B. To provide an independent view of the project

   C. The results of the review help the project manager to identify gaps in their own understanding

   D. To demonstrate how good the project manager is

2   **Which of these is not a type of project review?**

   A. Gate review

   B. Post-project review

   C. Benefits review

   D. Quantity review

3   **Project audits are carried out by:**

   A. The project sponsor

   B. An external party to the project

   C. The stakeholders

   D. The project manager's peers

4   **Post-project reviews happen:**

   A. After the project has been handed over but before closure

   B. After the project has been handed over and closed

   C. Before the project is handed over

   D. At the end of each project phase

5   **Between which phases will the gate review be carried out?**

A. Development and deployment

B. Concept and initiation

C. Handover and closeout

D. All of the above

6   **A decision gate is used to decide whether:**

A. The project is still viable and can be continued

B. The stakeholders want the project to progress

C. The project manager is delivering according to scope

D. All the key performance indicators have been met

CHAPTER 26

INFORMATION MANAGEMENT AND REPORTING

By the end of this chapter you should be able to:

- Outline the purpose and benefits of project information management
- Outline the purpose and benefits of project progress reporting
- Define information management
- List the different types of reporting

26.1 Project information management

Information management is a cyclic process involving collecting, storing, curation, distribution, archiving and destruction of project information.

Project management relies on the use of accurate and timely information to help with delivery and decision-making, etc. As information is generated on projects, it is important to devise methods for managing this information through appropriate **collection, storage, curation, dissemination, archiving** and **destruction**.

Projects usually generate lots of information and in various formats (soft and hard); some may be important, others may not. Regardless of the type of information, there will be a need to use an appropriate and secure method to collect relevant project information – for example, meeting minutes, emails, reports, drawings, online reports, etc. Some organisations have developed standards for information collection to ensure consistent information is collected at all times. As the project professional, you must exercise care in what information you collect and how this is collected.

Managing project information requires more than just collecting the information, there is an increasing emphasis on data protection and its importance. Project data once collected must be securely stored as appropriate with sufficient protocols on who can access such data. For example, access to specific project information could be restricted to only specific individuals. Sometimes projects may collect sensitive and personal information or commercial data.

The project professional should be aware of the implication of being negligent with sensitive project information and keep up to date with how the information can be shared. A lot more goes into managing project information in a way that enhances project success rather than becoming an impediment.

Collecting and storing information is fundamental to the success of the project. Additionally, making sense of the information collected for decision purposes is also crucial. What is the point in collecting and storing information which no one can make any sense of or find and use? This idea makes data or information curation very important.

A good understanding of how to deal with and manage the information generated by the project is an extremely important step to facilitating the success of any project. Data curation can simply be explained as making data and information useful for the users. It involves all the steps required to make project information useful.

Project management often involves sharing lots of project information between teams, individuals, organisations, etc. This is the aspect of project information management for disseminating the information. Some organisations have specific procedures for sharing and/or disseminating information, and as a project professional you must ensure project information is shared appropriately and within any specific guidelines.

Project information should be appropriately stored for future use and referencing. Information archiving will deal with how relevant project information can be archived and retrieved efficiently when required. There are specific guidelines for how long different information can be stored. This means that information no longer needed may have to be archived and not destroyed.

Where information destruction is needed, an appropriate and secure process should be followed to destroy such information.

Proper information management involves the following steps:

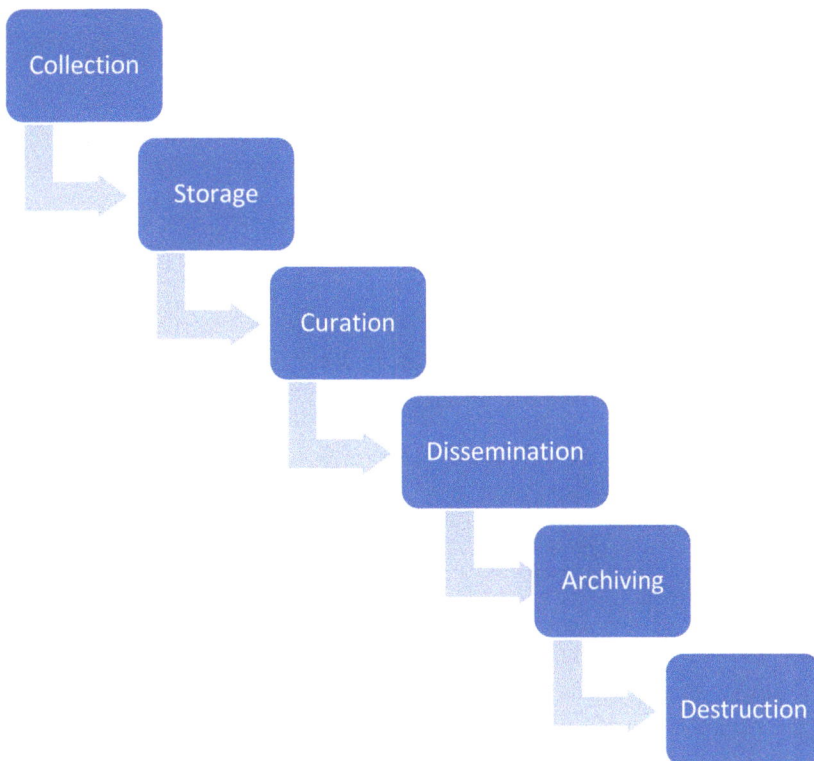

Figure 26.1 Project information management process

26.2 Reporting

Reporting is the presentation of information in a format that is appropriate and suitable for the intended audience.

Project reporting forms an important element of project management. The project manager uses various reporting methods to communicate the status of the project to the stakeholders, sponsor, superiors and to whom it may concern.

Different stakeholders may be interested in different aspects of the project or the status of the project at various stages.

Compiling appropriate, useful and timely reports is a key attribute and requirement for any project. It keeps the stakeholders up to date and informed.

Some reports require the project professional to establish a baseline to report against. In chapter eight the project baseline was discussed. Baselines tend to be the reference point to report against.

The next important step is the actual data collection element to compare with the baseline. For example, the project professional should find a way to measure the actual time and estimates and compare these to the baselines set at the onset of the project. This will serve as a good reporting measure as the project professional will use the available information to make an assessment which serves as a basis of providing a sound update to the key stakeholders.

26.3 The project manager may write/provide the following reports:

- Project status report: provides the most up-to-date status of the project. The project manager may address progress to date, cost spend to date, issues, changes, etc. The status report content may be tailored to suit the audience.
- Health and safety performance: near misses, accidents, injuries, etc.
- Hours worked on site
- Actual spend to date versus forecast spend
- Project risks report: this can be written to provide relevant stakeholders with an update on project risks. It may address risks which have occurred, their impact and/ or responses.

- Project board/executive reports, etc.: these will address relevant project information that the board may be interested in knowing.

Each report type conveys a different message tailored to the needs of the specific stakeholders/audience.

Project reporting can be in the form of an email, face-to-face update, presentation, etc. Whichever method is used should be appropriate and tailored to be effective and meet the needs of the stakeholders.

End-of-chapter assessment – project information management and reporting

Exercise 1 – The humanitarian mission project

Using the humanitarian mission project, prepare a status report updating the project sponsor as part of your regular reporting. What will you include in your report and why?

Exercise 2 – The humanitarian mission project

1   An example of a project report could be:

    A. A project status report

    B. A project risk report

    C. A project board report

    D. All of the above

2   Project reports can only be prepared by the project manager.

    A. True

    B. False

    C. Neither true nor false

    D. None of the above

3   Project reporting means taking project information and re-presenting it as the original, without any formatting, to ensure originality.

    A. True

    B. False

4   Which of these is not a characteristic of project reporting?

    A. Must always be appropriate

    B. Must always be useful

    C. Must always be relevant

    D. Must always be extensive

5   **Different reports convey different messages.**

A. True

B. False

6   **Which one of these is not a main reason for project reporting?**

A. It makes the project manager look professional

B. It provides an update on the project status to stakeholders

C. It keeps the stakeholder up to date

D. All of the above

APPENDIX 1

USEFUL CHECKLISTS

Useful checklist – concept stage

Have you thought about/discussed the expected benefits from the project idea/project need?	
Have you clearly written down these benefits and how you will measure them?	
Are you clear about what should be delivered/done (requirements) to achieve these benefits?	
Have you considered other options for providing the solution or solving the same problems?	
Are there specific functionalities and capabilities that these deliverables should have? Have you documented and obtained sign-off from all relevant parties (stakeholders)?	
Are you clear on what is and is not included in the project? Are these agreed and documented? (Do not assume.)	
Have you identified individuals/teams/organisations that may need to be consulted and engaged? Have you consulted and engaged them where appropriate?	
Have you selected a preferred option, and can you justify this in a business case where relevant?	
Have you estimated how much this option/idea will cost to implement? (May be a high-level estimate.)	
Is it worth spending on this option? Consider the risk, time and cost for implementing this option.	
Have you estimated how long it may take to implement this option given the risk involved?	
Have you considered the impact other internal and external factors might have on the project (political, economic, sociological, technical, legal and environmental)?	
Do you have enough information to justify why this project idea is worth the investment? Can you write the business case?	

Useful checklist – definition stage

Have you fully firmed up and documented the project deliverables and requirements?	
Have you prepared a project management plan? Does it address the main topics such as risk, cost, schedule, etc.?	
Have you planned how you will deal with changes that happen on the project?	
Have you planned how you will achieve/deliver products/services which are fit for purpose (quality management)?	
Have you planned how you will manage resources?	
Have you planned how you will communicate and who you will communicate with?	
Have you planned how you will manage and deal with unforeseen events (risks)?	
Have you planned how you will identify and manage all those interested in the project, whether positive or negative (stakeholders)?	
Have you identified the individual work packages/tasks required to deliver each deliverable (things to do)?	
Have you thought about how the individual works are linked to each other during delivery (scheduling)?	
Have you refined your costs and are confident of how much the project will cost?	
Have you thought about a contract? Do you need to have a contract/terms and conditions/agreement in place?	
Are all of the above covered in your project management plan (PMP) to support the delivery?	
Have you obtained sign-off of your PMP from the sponsor and relevant stakeholders?	

Useful checklist – deployment (execution) stage

Have you appointed a supplier/service providers/contractor?	
Have you agreed a suitable project start and end date?	
Have you checked everything to make sure you are ready to start? Do you have the appropriate authorisations in place to start the work?	
Are all relevant regulatory requirements in place? Have they been signed off?	
Have all relevant communications been sent out to the relevant stakeholders?	
Are plans in place to monitor and manage changes that will occur during implementation?	
Do you know how you will monitor the project to achieve the quality you expect?	
Do you have plans in place to monitor risks during delivery?	
Are you clear about the project objectives?	
Have you agreed the project schedule?	
Will the budget be enough for the project?	
Have you reviewed all risks?	
Have you agreed the project quality expectations?	
Do you have enough resources for the project?	

Useful checklist – transition (handover/closeout) stage

Are all deliverables/requirements completed as agreed at the start of the project?	
Do you have the list of all relevant individuals/teams to receive/accept the project for its beneficial use?	
Are there any certificates/operating manuals/commissioning notes to receive/provide?	
Have you prepared any completion notes where applicable?	
Do you have to carry out/receive any demonstrations/training, etc.?	
Do you have to arrange any site visits and inspections as part of the handover process?	
Do you have to issue/receive any warranty?	
Do you have a copy or list of all agreed changes just in case you must reference them?	
Have you documented lessons learned on the project?	
Do you have arrangements in place to deal with corrections that are needed post-handover?	
Are there any residual risks the client/users should be made aware of?	
Have you fulfilled all the contractual agreements?	
Have you informed the relevant stakeholders that the project is complete? Are they all happy for this project to be put into beneficial use?	
Have all the relevant paperwork for handover been signed off by the contractor/supplier and the relevant stakeholders?	

APPENDIX 2

STEP-BY-STEP GUIDE TO MANAGING A SIMPLE PROJECT
(CHAPTER-BY-CHAPTER GUIDE)

CONCEPT STAGE		Chapter	Page(s)
Step 1	Establish the need for the project (why)	Chapter 5	51-56
Step 2	Understand the roles and responsibilities and who may be involved in the project	Chapter 3	26-32
Step 3	Decide delivery approach (which life cycle)	Chapter 4	36-47
Step 4	Begin to prepare a high-level scope of what the project should deliver	Chapter 11	92-100
Step 5	Identify the factors that can influence how the project is delivered	Chapter 2	20-23
Step 6	Beware of the regulatory framework, laws, Acts, etc. which may impact on how the project is delivered	Chapter 24	196-199
Step 7	Begin to document some of the risks presented by the various project options being considered	Chapter 19	154-162
Step 8	Estimate the time and cost for each option being considered	Chapter 14	124-128
Step 9	Commence the stakeholder management process. First start with identification, and then analysis, to determine who may be interested or affected by the project and the level of influence or power they have	Chapter 6	57-62
Step 10	Be prepared to justify why the project or preferred option is the best one to progress to achieve the expected benefits	Chapter 7	65-68
DEVELOPMENT (PLANNING) STAGE		Chapter	Page(s)
Step 11	Begin to prepare the project delivery strategy (project management plan)	Chapter 8	71-76
Step 12	Refine the project scope outputs/outcomes (deliverables)	Chapter 11	92-100
Step 13	Refine the project requirement	Chapter 10	86-89

Step 14	Think about quality. Know/agree what you expect and how fit for purpose it should be. Avoid surprises and disappointments	Chapter 9	78-83
Step 15	Prepare to succeed. Define what a successful project will mean to you. Think about the conditions that will make a successful project	Chapter 13	118-121
Step 16	Carry out a detailed risk assessment presented by the project	Chapter 19	154-162
Step 17	Identify the things-to-do. Arrange these sequentially/concurrently for optimum delivery approach	Chapter 12	104-114
Step 18	Refine the estimates of the project time and cost and be sure of how much it will cost and how long it will take	Chapter 14	124-128
Step 19	Refine the project management plan and ensure that all the planning activities above are documented and that relevant baselines are documented	Chapter 8	71-75
Step 20	Procure the goods and services needed for the project	Chapter 18	149-152
Step 21	Agree an appropriate working relationship with the supplier/contractor where applicable (contract)	Chapter 18	149-152
DEPLOYMENT (DELIVERY) STAGE		**Chapter**	**Page(s)**
Step 22	Monitor progress on site	Chapter 26, Appendix 1 & All chapters	207-211, 214
Step 23	Monitor and manage changes	Chapter 16	136-140
Step 24	Monitor and manage issues	Chapter 20	165-167
Step 25	Monitor and manage risks	Chapter 19	154-162

Step 26	Monitor and manage configuration items	Chapter 15	131-134
Step 27	Monitor and manage quality	Chapter 9	78-83
Step 28	Monitor and manage project resources	Chapter 17	143-146
TRANSITION (HANDOVER & CLOSEOUT) STAGE		**Chapter**	**Page(s)**
Step 29	Handover and closeout	Chapters 4, 25, Appendix 1	46,202-204,218

APPENDIX 3

PROJECT EXAMPLES FOR GROUP DISCUSSIONS

Exercise 1	You are the manager of a team of 20 staff. You require a TV to be installed on the staffroom kitchen wall. This is an important 'need' because it came about as a result of a recent staff survey.
	As a senior leadership team member, you are also aware that the business's finances are tight. It may be very doubtful that the TV and the installation funding will be approved.
	You strongly believe that this project will benefit the staff in many ways.
	i. Prepare a simple justification for this project taking into consideration various options for meeting the need and the justification for the preferred option.
	ii. List some of the benefits you think this project will bring. Try grouping your benefits into direct/indirect benefits etc. and ensure they are also SMART.
Exercise 2	You have recently joined a new team as a junior project manager. This is your second week. Your line manager has asked you to assist with a proposed controversial project that is expected to draw a lot of opposition because of its controversies.
	Your manager is keen to start with the implementation as soon as possible, regardless. He believes the opposition will stop over time and therefore feels there is no need to waste a lot of time seeking stakeholders' views of carrying out further engagement.
	You have explained to your manager about the need to engage stakeholders appropriately. You have offered to assist with engaging the stakeholders.
	i. What will you do as a first approach in trying to engage your stakeholders?
	ii. How will you go about identifying the people, organisations, teams which may be affected?
	iii. What guidance can you give to your manager to assist with having a successful stakeholder engagement?

Exercise 3	You have been given the go-ahead to organise a charity sports event for school kids in your town. In all, you are expecting nearly one thousand 10-11-year-olds to attend from about 20 local schools. The event should be held in a local football stadium between 9am and 3pm.
	Following a recent incident with a similar event organised by another school, your manager has asked you to use your project management knowledge and experience to carry out a risk assessment ensuring all potential risks are covered.
	i. How will you go about preparing a risk register for this event?
	ii. Who will you involve in the risk identification process?
	iii. Prepare a risk register, identifying some of the risks, their probability, impact and mitigation, etc.
Exercise 4	You are part of a team tasked with introducing a new IT suite for your department. This project was trialled once but failed due to poor planning and implementation strategy.
	You have volunteered to assist the team with the planning and implementation. Your task is to prepare a work breakdown structure (to-do list) for the software implementation.
	i. Can you draft a work breakdown structure starting with the main deliverable and breaking it down into various sub-deliverables and subsequently smaller work packages for discussion?
Exercise 5	You want to build a small conservatory attached to your existing house. You have no construction experience, so you have invited several builders to come around to assess the work and provide you with an estimate/quotation. The builders have returned three estimates by text message, giving you the estimate as a ballpark figure.
	i. Using your estimating knowledge, how will you go about challenging the estimates to make sure they represent value for money?
	ii. You have some friends in the area who recently built similar conservatories but theirs were either much larger than yours or smaller. How can you make use of their knowledge and experience to help you understand the estimate you have? iii. You have decided to prepare your own estimate to compare with any quotations you receive. Which estimating technique will be useful and why?

Exercise 6	A project you are managing must change because one of the stakeholders has asked for some last-minute changes to the scope. You think this will cost extra money and possibly delay the project completion.
	The stakeholder has called you on the phone to say they will pay the difference when the project is complete. Given the time pressure, the stakeholder's director has also called to confirm that they will pay the difference.
	i. Is this enough for you to instruct the change?
	ii. Can you complete a change control form for the stakeholder to sign for your records?
	iii. What will you include in the change form?
	iv. Who should be the approver for this change?
Exercise 7	You have been asked to install a small smoking shelter outside your work canteen for staff use. A location has already been identified. You have been appointed as the project manager for this work.
	i. Split this project into phases and list three key activities you will undertake within each phase/stage.
	ii. Compile a stakeholder list for this project and use it to draw a stakeholder grid for discussion with your manager.
	iii. How will you go about agreeing the project requirements?
	iv. How will you ensure that this project will be fit for purpose?
	v. Can you come up with three criteria you will use to determine that the project is successful?
	vi. Can you identify five risks for this project, both during delivery and installation, and plan how you will respond to them?
Exercise 8	You have recently joined a new team as the head of projects following the retirement of the previous head. You are six months into your role and the project team is resentful, there is no cohesion within the team and the situation is becoming worse day by day.
	Some of the team members feel their skills are being undermined, others feel unappreciated. Overall, the team is not performing.

	You have been summoned by the leadership team to present to them what you think the issues are and how you plan to address these.
	i. As a project lead, outline some of the possible causes of these issues.
	ii. How do you think you can resolve these problems?
	iii. Do you think as a leader you must change or adapt your approach to suit the team?
Exercise 9	You are leading a fundraising event for your local charity. There are various stakeholders who may either be affected by this event or will be interested in it.
	i. Using a fictitious charity event, identify 10 stakeholders who may be interested or affected by this event.
	ii. Prepare a communication plan for your team to use in engaging the stakeholders.
Exercise 10	You have a need to carry out a piece of work to divide an existing office space into two separate rooms.
	This looks straightforward, so you are proposing to ask one of your work colleagues, who is also a part-time builder, to carry out this work in return for a couple of days off work. Having recently attended project management training, you are also concerned about health, safety and welfare arrangements.
	i. As a manager, what are some of your responsibilities and duties?
	ii. Is it okay to ask your work colleague to do this work? And if so, what arrangement will you put in place?
	iii. Would it be better to ask a professional to do the work? If so, what will you check to ensure the health, safety and welfare of everyone is secured?

Exercise 11	You are planning a wedding for your daughter and it feels like everything is all over the place. You feel overwhelmed with all the things you need to do. You want to employ a wedding planner but they are too expensive so you have agreed to plan and organise everything yourself.
	i. Using your project management knowledge, break the wedding planning and organisation into phases.
	ii. Within each phase, identify some of the activities you will undertake.
	iii. List some of the to-do items and use these to create a simple work breakdown structure.
Exercise 12	The head of your organisation's IT department has requested funding via email, requesting a large sum to improve the organisation's data compliance process because of recent breaches. You are also concerned that this is a critical issue that must be addressed immediately in order to comply with regulations however, you are not fully satisfied with how this justification has been prepared. As the project sponsor, what are some of the considerations you would want to see to be convinced that the project need has been carefully thought through?

ANSWER KEY

Chapter 1		Chapter 2		Chapter 3		Chapter 4		Chapter 5		Chapter 6		Chapter 7		Chapter 8		Chapter 9	
Q1.	B	Q1.	C	Q1	A	Q1	C	Q1	B	Q1	D	Q1	B	Q1	C	Q1	B
Q2	D	Q2	C	Q2	B	Q2	A	Q2	A	Q2	A	Q2	C	Q2	D	Q2	D
Q3	D	Q3	D	Q3	B	Q3	D	Q3	D	Q3	A	Q3	B	Q3	B	Q3	D
Q4	A	Q4	D	Q4	A	Q4	C	Q4	B	Q4	A	Q4	A	Q4	D	Q4	B
Q5	A	Q5	D	Q5	B	Q5	D	Q5	B	Q5	A	Q5	A	Q5	C	Q5	A
Q6	D	Q6	A	Q6	D	Q6	A	Q6	B	Q6	D	Q6	D	Q6	D	Q6	*
Q7	C	Q7	B	Q7	D	Q7	A	Q7	*	Q7	A	Q7	A	Q7	D	Q7	*
Q8	A	Q8	A	Q8	C	Q8	C	Q8	*	Q8	C	Q8	B	Q8	*	Q8	*
Q9	C	Q9		Q9	B	Q9	C	Q9	*	Q9	A	Q9	*	Q9	*	Q9	*
Q10	B	Q10		Q10	A	Q10	C	Q10	*	Q10		Q10	*	Q10		Q10	*

Chapter 10		Chapter 11		Chapter 12		Chapter 13		Chapter 14		Chapter 15		Chapter 16		Chapter 17		Chapter 18	
Q1.	A	Q1.	D	Q1	B	Q1	C	Q1	C	Q1	D	Q1	B	Q1	A	Q1	D
Q2	C	Q2	D	Q2	D	Q2	A	Q2	A	Q2	A	Q2	D	Q2	D	Q2	C
Q3	D	Q3	A	Q3	A	Q3	D	Q3	C	Q3	A	Q3	B	Q3	B	Q3	C
Q4	C	Q4	C	Q4	B	Q4	D	Q4	C	Q4	A	Q4	C	Q4	D	Q4	A
Q5	*	Q5	C	Q5	C	Q5	B	Q5	B	Q5	D	Q5	B	Q5	A	Q5	*
Q6	*	Q6	A	Q6	D	Q6	*	Q6	C	Q6		Q6	C	Q6	A	Q6	*
Q7	*	Q7	B	Q7	D	Q7	*	Q7	*	Q7		Q7	B	Q7	B	Q7	*
Q8	*	Q8	B	Q8	A	Q8	*	Q8	*	Q8		Q8	B	Q8	A	Q8	*
Q9	*	Q9	C	Q9	B	Q9	*	Q9	*	Q9		Q9	D	Q9		Q9	*
Q10	*	Q10	D	Q10	C	Q10	*	Q10	*	Q10		Q10	*	Q10		Q10	*

Chapter 19		Chapter 20		Chapter 21		Chapter 22		Chapter 23		Chapter 24		Chapter 25		Chapter 26	
Q1.	A	Q1.	B	Q1	B	Q1	C	Q1	D	Q1	C	Q1	D	Q1	D
Q2	A	Q2	A	Q2	A	Q2	D	Q2	A	Q2	D	Q2	D	Q2	B
Q3	D	Q3	A	Q3	D	Q3	D	Q3	A	Q3	C	Q3	B	Q3	B
Q4	A	Q4	D	Q4	D	Q4	B	Q4	A	Q4	A	Q4	A	Q4	D
Q5	D	Q5		Q5	A	Q5	B	Q5	D	Q5	B	Q5	A	Q5	A
Q6	*	Q6		Q6	D	Q6		Q6	C	Q6		Q6	A	Q6	A
Q7	*	Q7		Q7	D	Q7		Q7	C	Q7		Q7	*	Q7	
Q8	*	Q8		Q8	B	Q8		Q8	A	Q8		Q8	*	Q8	
Q9	*	Q9		Q9	D	Q9		Q9	*	Q9		Q9	*	Q9	
Q10	*	Q10		Q10	*	Q10		Q10	*	Q10		Q10	*	Q10	

GLOSSARY

A

Accept – a response to a threat where no course of action is taken.

Acceptance criteria – requirements and essential conditions that must be achieved before a deliverable is accepted.

Activity – a task, job, operation or process consuming time and possibly other resources.

Activity duration – the length of time it takes to complete an activity.

Actual expenditure – the costs that have been charged to the budget and for which payment has been made or accrued.

Analogous estimating – an estimating technique based on the comparison with, and factoring from, the cost of similar, previous work.

Assumptions – statements taken for granted or truth.

Audit – systematic retrospective examination of the whole, or part, of a project or function to measure conformance with predetermined standards, e.g. financial audit, project audit, health and safety audit, etc.

B

Baseline – the reference levels against which a project, programme or portfolio is monitored and controlled.

Benefit – positive and measurable impact resulting from the delivery of a project.

Benefits management – the identification, definition, planning, tracking and realisation of benefits.

Benefit realisation – the practice of ensuring that benefits are derived from outputs and outcomes.

Bottom-up estimating – an estimation technique that uses detailed specifications to estimate time and cost for each product or activity.

Breakdown structure – a hierarchical structure used for breaking down project activities are broken down or decomposed, e.g. work breakdown structure (WBS), cost breakdown structure (CBS) and organisational breakdown structure (OBS).

Brief – the output of the concept phase of a project or programme.

Business as usual – an organisation's normal day-to-day operations.

Business case – provides justification for undertaking a project or programme. It evaluates the benefits, costs and risks of alternative options and provides a rationale for the preferred option.

C

Change control - the process for controlling project change requests to alter any approved baseline of cost, time etc. Change control ensures changes are captured, evaluated, approve, rejected or deferred where applicable.

Change freeze – a point after which no further changes to scope are allowed.

Change log – a registeror record of all project changes; proposed, authorised or rejected.

Change management – structured approach to moving an organisation from the current state to the desired future state.

Change register – a record of all proposed changes to scope.

Change request – a request to obtain formal approval for changes to the scope of work.

Client – the party to a contract who commissions the work and pays for it on completion.

Closeout – the completion of work on a project.

Communication is the process or an act of transferring information and ensuring that there is a common understanding. Communication can be written, verbal, non-verbal or virtual.

Concept – the first phase in the project life cycle. During this phase the problem, need or opportunity is confirmed, the overall feasibility of the work is considered, and a preferred solution is identified.

Configuration – functional and physical characteristic of a product as defined in its specification.

Configuration management encompasses the technical and administrative activities concerned with the creation, maintenance, controlled change and quality control of the scope of work.

Consumable resource – a type of resource that only remains available until consumed. Context – a collective term for the governance and setting of a project.

Contingency – a resource set aside for responding to identified risks.

Contract - legal agreement made between two or more parties. Contracts are usually legally enforceable and sets out the commitments and responsibilities of the parties involved.

Contractor – a person, company, or firm which holds a contract for carrying out the works and/or the supply of goods in connection with the project.

Cost breakdown structure – hierarchical breakdown of a project into cost elements.

Cost estimating – the process of predicting the costs of a project.

Critical path - the series of activities within a network from start to finish that determines the total project duration.

Critical success factor – a factor considered to be most conducive to the achievement of a successful project.

Customer – any person who defines needs or wants, justifies or pays for part or the entire project, or evaluates or uses the results. This could be the client, owner, employer, etc.

D

Deliverables – a product, set of products or package of work that will be delivered to, and formally accepted by, a stakeholder.

Duration – the length of time needed to complete a project or activity.

E

Enhance – a response to an opportunity that increases its probability or impact, or both.

Environment – the circumstances and conditions within which the project must operate.

Estimate is the approximation of how much a project, activity, or work will cost or how long it will take to complete.

Estimating is the use of different methods, approaches, and techniques to approximate the project cost and time.

Estimating funnel – a representation of the increasing levels of estimating accuracy that can be achieved through the phases of the life cycle.

Exploit – a response to an opportunity that maximises both its probability and impact.

EXTENDED life cycle - like any standard life cycle (linear, iterative) that extends to include additional phases of

adopting the project into business as usual to realise the project benefits and through to disposal.

F

Finish to Finish – a dependency in an activity on a node network. It indicates one activity cannot finish until the other activity has finished.

Finish to Start – a dependency in an activity on a node network. It indicates one activity cannot start until the other activity has finished.

Float – a term used to describe the flexibility with which an activity may be rescheduled.

Free float - the amount of time a task or activity can be delayed, rescheduled, or extended without delaying the start of the succeeding activity

Funding – the means by which the capital required to undertake the project is secured and then made available as required.

G

Gantt chart – a graphical representation of activity against time.

Gate – the point between phases, gates and/or tranches where a go/no-go decision can be made about the remainder of the work.

H

Handover – the point in the life cycle where deliverables are handed over to the sponsor or users.

Hybrid life cycle – the approach combines the benefits of both the linear and iterative life cycles to create this new life cycle

I

Information management - a cyclic process involving collecting, storing, curation, distribution, archiving and destruction of project information.

Issue - problem that has happened on the project for which the project manager is unable to deal with by themselves. Project issues should usually be escalated for resolution.

ITERATIVE project life cycle makes allowance for some of the project stages to be repeated severally to get right prior to progressing to the subsequent stages. This allows better understanding of the project objective and scope

K

Key performance indicators (KPIs) - specific measures the project will use to determine if the project is meeting or is likely to meet its planned objectives. KPI is used to determine how well the project is performing towards a successful end

L

Latest finish – the latest possible time by which an activity has to finish within the logical activity and imposed constraints of the network, without affecting the total project duration.

Leadership - the ability of an individual, an organisation, group, or team to be

able to establish a vision influence and guide other individuals, teams, organisations towards that vision.

Lessons learned – documented experiences that can be used to improve future management of projects.

Life cycle – simply defines the distinct stages of a project. It is used to provide a structure for undertaking the project and governing it effectively.

LINEAR project life cycle - associated with projects that are delivered by following a straight and unidirectional sequence. For example, from the initial concept through to implementation and handover of the project.

Logical relationships – based on the dependency between two project activities or between a project activity and a milestone.

M

Milestone - an important event or date in the project.

Mobilisation – the bringing together of project personnel and securing equipment and facilities. This is carried out during the project start-up phase.

N

Need, problem, opportunity – the underlying reason for undertaking a project. Without a definable need, problem or opportunity, a project should not go ahead. Network diagram – a pictorial presentation of project data in which the project logic is the main determinant of the placement of the activities in the diagram. Sometimes called the flowchart, logic drawing, activity network or logic diagram.

O

Opportunity – a positive risk event that, if it occurs, will have a beneficial effect on the achievement of objectives.

Organisational breakdown structure (OBS) – hierarchical way in which the organisation may be divided into management levels and groups, for planning and control purposes.

P

Parametric estimating – an estimating technique that uses a statistical relationship between historic data and other variables to calculate an estimate.

Performance – the quality of the delivery and the deliverables (outputs) of the project. Phase – a major subdivision of a life cycle.

Phase review – a review that takes place at the end of a life cycle phase. See gate review.

Planning – the process of identifying the means, resources and actions necessary to accomplish an objective.

Planning stage – the stage prior to the implementation stage when product activity, resources and quality plans are produced.

Portfolio - the totality of all the projects, programmes, and business, as usual, an organisation can select, prioritise, and

deliver to meet their overall strategic objective.

Portfolio management - the totality of all the projects, programmes, and business, as usual, an organisation can select, prioritise, and deliver to meet their overall strategic objective.

Post-implementation review – a review between 6-12 months after a system in a project has met its objectives to verify that it continues to meet user requirements.

Predecessor – an activity that must be completed (or partially completed) before a specified activity can begin. Process – a set of interrelated resources and activities that transform input into outputs.

Procurement - how goods, services, or works are sourced from an external party to incorporate or use on the project. Procurement will also involve contract arrangement and execution and managing the relationship with the suppliers.

Procurement strategy - the high-level and an overarching approach an organisation will use to purchase goods, services or works from external suppliers. The strategy may include a strategy for selecting service providers or managing the relationships.

Programme - a group of related projects, including business as usual activities together. A programme results in a change that is strategically beneficial to an organisation

Programme management - the management of a group of related projects, including business as usual activities together. A programme results in a change that is strategically beneficial to an organisation.

Project - activity that is temporary and undertaken to bring about a notable or unique change. The change should ultimately lead to benefits.

Project board – the body to which the project manager is accountable for achieving the project objectives. See steering group.

Project closure – formal termination of a project at any point during its life.

Project environment – the context within which the project is formulated, assessed and realised. This includes all external factors that have an impact on the project.

Project initiation – the beginning of a project at which point certain management activities are required to ensure that the project is established with clear reference terms and adequate management structure.

Project management - the application of processes, methods, knowledge, skills and experience to achieve specific objectives for change.

Project management plan (PMP) – the output of a definition phase of a project. Provider – a person or company that provides goods or services.

Q

Quality - the fitness for purpose or the degree of conformance of the outputs of a process or the process itself to the requirements.

Quality assurance consists of inspections, measurements, testing, and procedures followed during the delivery process to ensure that the project outputs meet acceptance criteria defined during quality planning.

Quality control – the process of monitoring specific project results to determine if they comply with the relevant standards and identifying ways to eliminate causes of unsatisfactory performance.

Quality management – The discipline for ensuring the outputs, benefits and the processes by which they are delivered, meet stakeholder requirements and are fit for purpose.

Quality planning takes the defined scope and specifies the acceptance criteria used to validate that the outputs are fit for purpose to the sponsor

R

Reduce – a response to a threat that reduces its probability, impact, or both.

Reject – a response to an opportunity where no action is taken.

Reporting – is the presentation of information in a format that is appropriate and suitable for the intended audience

Request for change – a proposal by the project manager for a change to the project as a result of a project issue report.

Requirements - are all the things that are wanted or needed by the stakeholders, customers, users, clients, etc. These can be defined and categorised using the must-haves, should-haves, could-haves, and won't-haves of the project.

Resource levelling – a scheduling calculation that delays activities such that resource usage is kept below specified limits. It is also known as resource limited scheduling.

Resource management - the process by which all the required resources needed for the project are acquired internally or externally and used on the project.

Resource scheduling – a collection of techniques used to calculate the resources required to deliver the work and when they will be required.

Resource smoothing – a scheduling calculation that involves utilising float or increasing or decreasing the resources required for specific activities such that any peaks and troughs of resource usage are smoothed out. This does not affect the overall duration. It is also known as time-limited resource scheduling.

Risk - the probability of something happening on the project such that it can affect all or some of the project objectives from being achieved

Risk assessment – an assessment and synthesis of risk events to gain an understanding of their individual significance and their combined impact on objectives. Risk event – an uncertain event or set of circumstances that would, if it/they occurred, have an effect on the achievement of one or more objectives.

Risk management is the process that allows project risks to be proactively identified, analysed, and responded to effectively.

Risk management plan – a document defining how project risk analysis and management are to be implemented in the context of a particular project.

Risk owner – the person who has responsibility for dealing with a particular risk on a project and for identifying and managing responses.

Risk register – a document listing identified risk events and their corresponding planned responses.

Risk response – an action or set of actions to reduce the probability or impact of a threat, or to increase the probability or impact of an opportunity.

S

Schedule - the timetable for showing the planned start and finish dates for project activities or events.

Scope - the project deliverables and the amount of work involved in achieving them.

Scope management - the process for finding, clarifying, and controlling the project deliverables.

Sponsor – an individual or body for whom the project is undertaken and who is the primary risk taker.

Stakeholders - individuals, teams, groups, or an organisation that may be interested, affected, or play a role in the project.

Steering group – a body established to monitor the project and give guidance to the project sponsor or project manager.

Success criteria - the yardstick used to determine the clients, users, customers, and stakeholders' requirements have been met.

Success factors - the necessary conditions, practices, and environment essential for the project to be successful.

T

Task – the smallest indivisible part of an activity when it is broken down to a level best understood and performed by a specific person or organisation.

Team - a group of individuals working collaboratively towards achieving a common goal.

Teamwork – a group of people working in collaboration or by cooperation towards a common goal.

Threat – a negative risk event; a risk event that, if it occurs, will have a detrimental effect on the objectives.

Three-point estimate – an estimation in which optimistic, most likely, and pessimistic values are given.

Timeboxing – commonly used in the interative life cycle approach. Project iterations are fixed to an end date which is not allowed to change. This ensures iterations do not result in project delays

Total float - the amount of time a task or activity can be delayed, rescheduled or extended without affecting the total project duration (end date).

Transfer – a response to a threat that reduces its probability, impact, or both, by transferring the risk to a third party.

U

Uncertainty – a state of incomplete knowledge about a proposition. Usually associated with risks – both threats and opportunities.

User requirements – the requirements governing the project's deliverables or products as expressed by the user. What the user needs expressed in user terminology.

Users – the group of people who are intended to benefit from the project or operate the deliverables.

V

Version control – the recording and management of the configuration of different versions of the project's products.

W

Work breakdown structure (WBS) – a way in which a project may be divided by level into discrete groups for programming, cost planning and control purposes.

Work package – a group of related activities that are defined at the same level within a work breakdown structure.

X No items defined.

Y No items defined.

Z No items defined.

REFERENCES

Association for Project Management (2012) *APM Body of Knowledge*. 6th ed. Princes Risborough, England: Association for Project Management.

Baldwin, B. and Hock, C. (2004) *The financial reporting project and readings*. 4th ed. Florence, AL: South-Western College Publishing.

Buttrick, R. (2018) *The project workout: The ultimate guide to directing and managing business-led projects*. London, England: Routledge.

Center for Creative Leadership (CCL), Kanaga, K. and Browning, H. (2011) *Maintaining Team Performance*. 1st ed. Pfeiffer.

Griffith, B. A. and Dunham, E. B. (2014) *Working in teams: Moving from high potential to high performance*. Thousand Oaks, CA: SAGE Publications.

Kouzes, J. M. and Posner, B. Z. (2016) *Learning leadership: The five fundamentals of becoming an exemplary leader*. Edited by J. M. Kouzes and B. Z. Posner. Nashville, TN: John Wiley & Sons. doi: 10.1002/9781119176725.

Lindgreen, A. (2018) *Engaging with stakeholders: A relational perspective on responsible business*. Routledge.

Munier, N. (2014) *Risk management for engineering projects: Procedures, methods and tools*. 2014th ed. Cham, Switzerland: Springer International Publishing.

Murray-Webster, R., Dalcher, D. and Association for Project Management (2019) *APM body of knowledge*. 7th ed. Princes Risborough, England: Association for Project Management.

Murray-Webster, R. and Simon, P. (2006) *Starting Out in Project Management*. Princes Risborough, England: Association for Project Management.

Office of Government Commerce (2006) *Business Benefits Through Programme and Project Management*. Norwich, England: Stationery Office Books.

Scott, A. (2014) *MSC study guide APMP - the APM project management qualification*. Royal Tunbridge Wells, England: Management Skills Centre.

Simon, P. and etc. (eds.) (1997) *Project risk analysis and management guide: PRAM*. High Wycombe, England: APM Group.

Taylor, J. C. (2005) *Project cost estimating: Tools, techniques and perspectives*. London, England: St Lucie Press.

The nine Belbin Team Roles (no date) *Belbin.com*. Available at: http://www.belbin.com/about/belbin-team-roles/ (Accessed: October 7, 2020).

Warren, L. (2013) *Procurement in practice: Avoiding the pitfalls and getting the best result*. London, England: National Housing Federation.

INDEX

www.ingramcontent.com/pod-product-compliance
Lightning Source LLC
Chambersburg PA
CBHW050105220326
41598CB00043B/7388